TO

_____

FROM

_____

DATE

_____

VeggieTales

GROWING with GOD

365 Daily Devos for Boys

ISBN-13: 978-1-68397-036-1 (paperback)
ISBN-13: 978-1-68397-035-4 (padded hardcover)

Published by WorthyKids/Ideals, an imprint of Worthy Publishing Group, a division of Worthy Media, Inc., Nashville, Tennessee.
WorthyKids/Ideals is a registered trademark of Worthy Media, Inc.

Printed and bound in China

RRD-SZ_Jul17_1

VeggieTales

GROWING with GOD

365 Daily Devos for Boys

A MESSAGE TO PARENTS

As a parent, you know the importance of teaching your children the big ideas that are found in God's Holy Word. The daily devotions in this book will help you do that.

Each devotion contains a Bible verse and a kid-friendly essay on an important topic such as honesty, forgiveness, or kindness. Also included is a question or thought to reinforce the day's lesson, and a daily prayer will help your son to develop a habit of talking to God.

During the coming year, read a devotion from this book with your son every day. This will help him establish a daily practice of hearing from God. It will also give you 365 different opportunities to share God's love and wisdom with your son, and a daily chance to remind him that God made him special and He wants him to grow in His love.

SHARE GOD'S LOVE

"If you have two shirts, share with the person who does not have one. If you have food, share that too."

Luke 3:11 ICB

God talks a lot in the Bible about sharing and giving. It's really important to Him that we take care of one another—especially those who don't have everything they need, like food and clothing and a safe place to live.

You may not think you can make a big difference, but you can! If you ask God to show you how you can share with others, He will show you what to do.

Even a small act of kindness can change a person's life. Share God's love everywhere you go!

THOUGHT OF THE DAY

Who do you know—either a grown-up or a kid—who could use your help?

PRAY TODAY

Dear God, I want to do whatever I can to help people and show them how much You love them. Amen.

FINDING WISDOM

For wisdom is far more valuable than rubies. Nothing you desire can compare with it.

Proverbs 8:11 NLT

The Bible tells us about a king named Solomon. He had a chance to ask God for anything in the world! But he didn't ask for money or power. Solomon asked for wisdom. He knew that the most important thing he could do was to make wise choices.

Do you know that you can be like King Solomon? Whenever you aren't sure what to do, just ask God to help you. He promises to give you wisdom too! As long as you ask God for wisdom and do your best to follow what He says, you can count on making great choices!

THOUGHT OF THE DAY

Can you think of a time you made a wise choice?

PRAY TODAY

Dear God, I want to be wise and make good choices. Please help me remember to ask You for help every day. Amen.

DO YOUR BEST

Let your patience show itself perfectly in what you do. Then you will be perfect and complete and will have everything you need.

James 1:4 NCV

Everyone has work they need to do. Maybe you have chores at home, like cleaning your room or setting the table for dinner. Maybe you help out with a younger brother or sister. And maybe you go to school, where you are learning new things every day. Whatever you do, God wants you to do your best.

Doing your best doesn't mean being perfect. You make God happy when you take your time, try hard, and enjoy what you're doing. And when you see that you've done a good job, you'll feel happy too!

THOUGHT OF THE DAY

How can you do your best at something today?

PRAY TODAY

Dear God, please help me work hard at everything I do. I want to do good work! Amen.

A GREAT GIFT!

Let us give thanks all the time to God through Jesus Christ. Our gift to Him is to give thanks. Our lips should always give thanks to His name.

Hebrews 13:15 NLV

God has given you so many gifts! He's blessed you with family and friends, a cozy home, and good food to eat. In fact, every day is God's loving gift to you. And guess what? You can give God something, too—the gift of praise!

There are so many ways to praise God. You can tell Him how much you love him, share His wonderful love with others, or even sing Him a song! Pick a favorite song from church or make up one that is all your own. God loves to receive your unique praise!

THOUGHT OF THE DAY
Look for ways to praise God every day!

PRAY TODAY
Dear God, I praise You for all the blessings You've given me. Thank You for Your amazing love! Amen.

SERVE THE LORD

Do not be lazy but work hard, serving the Lord with all your heart.

Romans 12:11 NCV

The Bible says it over and over again: it's important to serve other people. Serving can mean many different things. You can help your mom clean the house. You could help a friend with her homework. You could participate in a fundraiser for a special cause. You could write a letter to someone in your family whom you don't see very often. Whatever God leads you to do, work hard, and He will bless you!

THOUGHT OF THE DAY

It sounds strange, but it's true: the more you serve others, the better it makes you feel.

PRAY TODAY

Dear God, I want to do what I can to serve others. Please show me what You want me to do, and I will do it with all my heart. Amen.

GOD'S PROTECTION

For he will order his angels to protect you wherever you go.

Psalm 91:11 NLT

God loves you so much that He never lets you out of His sight. And He sends His angels to guard you and keep you safe, no matter where you go.

It's important that we make wise choices so we don't get hurt by doing foolish things, but it's wonderful to know God and His angels will be with us no matter what!

THOUGHT OF THE DAY

Remember to pray every day and thank God for keeping you safe.

PRAY TODAY

Dear God, thank You for protecting me and keeping me safe. Amen.

A HOME FILLED WITH LOVE

But Ruth said, "Don't beg me to leave you or to stop following you. Where you go, I will go. Where you live, I will live. Your people will be my people, and your God will be my God."

Ruth 1:16 NCV

What makes a family? Love.

The Bible tells the story of Ruth, a special girl who really knew how to love her family. Ruth's husband died, but she chose to stay with her mother-in-law and take care of her, no matter what.

Ruth worked hard, and God rewarded her for her faithfulness. He gave Ruth a new husband and children, and one of Ruth's descendants was Jesus.

Love your family the way that Ruth loved hers, and you will be blessed!

THOUGHT OF THE DAY

What are three things you can do to help your home stay filled with love?

PRAY TODAY

Dear God, help me remember that next to You, my family should always come first. Thank You for blessing us. Amen.

GOD'S WAY

A gentle answer will calm a person's anger, but an unkind answer will cause more anger.

Proverbs 15:1 NCV

Sometimes when you are feeling angry, it's hard to say something in a gentle way. God wants you to handle your feelings His way. So take a deep breath and ask Him to help you say something kind.

God's way is full of peace, kindness, and love. Anger can make you say or do things that are not very peaceful or loving. The Bible tells us how we should act when we feel angry. You can always trust God to be with you and help you with your feelings.

THOUGHT OF THE DAY

Let God help you with your feelings.

PRAY TODAY

Dear God, help me to calm down and say kind words if I feel angry. Amen.

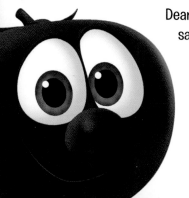

SOMETHING GOOD

And we know that for those who love God all things work together for good, for those who are called according to his purpose.

Romans 8:28 ESV

Have you ever wanted something very, very much? Maybe you wanted a new game or to visit the zoo. If these things didn't happen, were you disappointed?

God says all things work together for our good when we follow Him—*all things!* That means God can turn a disappointment around! He has great plans for you, and even though you might not understand everything when it happens, you can be sure that God loves you very much. And He can turn everything that happens into something good in your life.

THOUGHT OF THE DAY

God has something good for you today!

PRAY TODAY

Dear God, I don't understand why things go wrong sometimes, but I am so glad You can make them right. Amen.

A PROMISE OF LOVE

His banner over me was love.

Song of Solomon 2:4 KJV

God makes lots of amazing promises in the Bible, but the biggest one of all is that He will love you. No matter what. Forever. And it's a promise He will keep.

No matter where you are (and no matter what you have done), you can never lose God's love. It might be hard to understand that with your head, so just believe Him and receive His love with your heart.

You are God's special child. His love will always be there for you—no matter what!

THOUGHT OF THE DAY

God shows His love for you in a million ways, big and small. Can you think of three you noticed today?

PRAY TODAY

Dear God, the Bible teaches me that You are my loving Father. Thank You for loving me so much. Amen.

BE WISE, ACT WISELY

Are there those among you who are truly wise and understanding? Then they should show it by living right and doing good things with a gentleness that comes from wisdom.

James 3:13 NCV

If you want to be wise, you can start by being a good listener. Pay attention when your parents and teachers speak to you. Ask lots of questions if you don't understand something. Learn Bible stories that show you what God is like.

But don't forget to act on what you learn! Wisdom doesn't mean being smarter than everyone. Wisdom means using what you've learned to follow God's rules and show love to everyone. Wise people also understand that they don't know everything, but God does. So ask God for the wisdom you need. He will give it to you!

THOUGHT OF THE DAY

True wisdom comes from following God every day!

PRAY TODAY

Dear God, help me learn more about You so I can make wise choices! Amen.

JUST BELIEVE!

"Don't be afraid. Only believe."

Mark 5:36 HCSB

D o you remember the story of Daniel in the lions' den? Daniel, who loved and obeyed God, was thrown in a hole to be lunch for the hungry lions! But God protected him, and everything turned out better than it was before!

Hopefully, you'll never be in a situation quite like that. But is there something that frightens you or makes you afraid you will fail? God says don't be afraid! Just believe Him and do your best. He'll take care of the rest!

THOUGHT OF THE DAY

You can't be too afraid to try if you want to do great things!

PRAY TODAY

Dear God, thank You for taking care of me so I don't have to be afraid. I choose to believe You! Amen.

THE LIGHT ALWAYS WINS

The light shines in the darkness, and the darkness has never put it out.

John 1:5 GNT

What happens when you shine a flashlight in a dark place? The darkness goes away! The Bible says that Jesus is the light of the world, and when we bring Him into a dark place, the darkness goes away.

When friends don't get along, things can seem dark. When someone is sad, that can also feel like a dark place. Ask Jesus to help you say kind words and show His love, bringing light into the dark places around you. When you choose to share God's light and love, the darkness goes away! The light of Jesus always wins!

THOUGHT OF THE DAY

The love of Jesus shines a light to make the darkest places bright!

PRAY TODAY

Dear God, thank You for being the light of the world. Please help me share Your light with others every day. Amen.

LOOK ON THE BRIGHT SIDE

A happy heart makes the face cheerful, but heartache crushes the spirit.

Proverbs 15:13 NIV

Have you ever had a day when everything is going great? How about a day when everything seems to go wrong? The Bible says that if we have a happy heart, we can enjoy life—even when our day isn't going the way we want.

If the rain spoils your picnic, you can splash in the puddles! What if your friend can't come over to play? Maybe you can make up a new game with your toys. Instead of getting angry when things go wrong, find something to be glad about. That's called looking on the bright side!

THOUGHT OF THE DAY

How can you look on the bright side the next time things don't go the way you want?

PRAY TODAY

Dear God, I know bad things happen sometimes. When they do, please help me to look on the bright side. Amen.

GOD IS LOOKING AFTER YOU!

*The LORD is my light and my salvation; Whom shall I fear?
The LORD is the strength of my life; Of whom shall I be
afraid?*

Psalm 27:1 NKJV

Sometimes you may feel afraid. Everyone does. It's pretty normal. But the Bible tells us that with God we don't have to be afraid. He's bigger and stronger than anything that might make you scared!

Thankfully, God never leaves you, not even for a moment. He's always there to protect you.

God keeps His promises, and He wants you to trust Him completely. When you do, you don't have to be afraid.

THOUGHT OF THE DAY

Be brave! You and God together can handle anything!

PRAY TODAY

Dear God, thank You for always watching out for me and keeping me safe. Thank You for keeping my family safe too. Amen.

READY AND WAITING

Rejoice always! Pray constantly.

1 Thessalonians 5:16-17 HCSB

Lots of people pray at special times, like at bedtime or before meals. But God says we should pray all the time. What does that mean?

God wants you to feel very close to Him, and the best way to do that is to talk to Him all through your day. So when something makes you happy, tell God right away! If you feel confused, ask God to help you. If you feel sad, pray for God's comfort. He's always with you! You don't have to wait for a special time of day to talk to God.

THOUGHT OF THE DAY

God can't wait to hear what you're thinking about!

PRAY TODAY

Dear God, thank You for listening to my prayers anytime, anywhere! Amen.

PLAY FAIR AND WIN!

Happiness comes to those who are fair to others and are always just and good.

Psalm 106:3 TLB

Everyone enjoys winning games. It can even be tempting to do something that will help you win unfairly. But that's not really winning.

God wants us to play fair because it's right and kind. Cheating robs others of a good game! Instead, practice having a positive attitude whether you win or lose. If you win, thank everyone for playing with you and tell them you had fun. If you lose, you can congratulate the winner and ask to play again sometime. Everyone likes to play with someone who plays fair and keeps things fun!

THOUGHT OF THE DAY

Win or lose, you can still have a lot of fun!

PRAY TODAY

Dear God, help me resist the temptation to cheat. Give me a good attitude, whether or not I win. Amen.

A JOYFUL GIVER

God loves the person who gives happily.

2 Corinthians 9:7 ICB

God is so happy when you share your time and things with others. It's a great way to praise Him and get to know Him better. But don't just give—give happily!

Giving to others should make us glad because we're doing what God wants. We're also meeting new people and learning about them, which is fun! Be careful not to give with the goal of getting something back. Instead, give with a kind and open heart, excited to see what God does. When you give happily, God can do amazing things through you!

THOUGHT OF THE DAY

There are lots of ways to give to others. Find one that makes you happy!

PRAY TODAY

Dear God, thank You for my blessings. Help me share them joyfully! Amen.

MAKE THINGS RIGHT

Be kind and compassionate to one another, forgiving each other, just as in Christ God forgave you.

Ephesians 4:32 NIV

Have you ever hurt someone's feelings? Maybe you wouldn't share with a friend or you were rude to your mother. The best way to fix this is to ask for forgiveness!

God wants you to be kind and respectful of others. If you've hurt someone, whether by accident or on purpose, the right thing to do is take responsibility and ask for forgiveness. And sometimes that starts with saying "I'm sorry."

It isn't always easy to ask for forgiveness, especially if you're feeling angry or embarrassed. But if you do, you will be choosing love, just like God wants!

THOUGHT OF THE DAY

We can forgive because God forgives us!

PRAY TODAY

Dear God, help me to be kind and compassionate to others just like You are to me. Amen.

KEEP BURNING!

Don't burn out; keep yourselves fueled and aflame. Be alert servants of the Master, cheerfully expectant. Don't quit in hard times; pray all the harder.

Romans 12:11-12 MSG

School, sports, lessons, and time with friends are fun and important. But sometimes we can get so busy that we don't spend time with God or talk to God.

Talking with God will help you to follow His ways. Thanking Him for your blessings will also help you enjoy your life. You might even feel like you have more energy! God will help you keep your energy going so you can keep shining His love in the world and in your heart as you talk to Him each day.

THOUGHT OF THE DAY

Make sure to make time for your relationship with God. Remember that God is most important!

PRAY TODAY

Dear God, help me to spend time with You every day. Nothing is more important than our friendship! Amen.

GOD DREAMS BIG

Now glory be to God, who by his mighty power at work within us is able to do far more than we would ever dare to ask or even dream of—infinitely beyond our highest prayers, desires, thoughts, or hopes.

Ephesians 3:20 TLB

Do you have big dreams about what you want to be or do when you grow up? It's great for you to think about these things! But God has even bigger dreams for you—more than you can ever imagine, ask for, or think of on your own.

God has so much planned for you, and He is going to do everything needed for these things to happen in your life. All you have to do is spend time with God and listen to what He wants you to do. So listen up . . . because God dreams really big!

THOUGHT OF THE DAY

Think of a time when you were surprised with more than you could possibly imagine. What happened?

PRAY TODAY

Dear God, thank You for having such big dreams for me. I can't wait to see them come true! Amen.

A PEACEFUL FAMILY

How wonderful, how beautiful, when brothers and sisters get along!

Psalm 133:1 MSG

Do you ever feel frustrated at home? It happens to all of us! Maybe you have a brother or sister who gets into your things sometimes. Even though you love them very much, it's not unusual to argue now and then.

A home full of anger is no fun. So if you find yourself arguing, ask God to help you bring peace to the situation instead. That might mean suggesting something different that everyone can agree on, or sometimes being willing to give up what you want to do. Seeking peace is a good thing, and sometimes you have to work at it.

THOUGHT OF THE DAY
A peaceful home means more room for fun!

PRAY TODAY
Dear God, please help me seek Your peace, even when I feel frustrated. Amen.

ONE THING AT A TIME

Tell me in the morning about your love, because I trust you. Show me what I should do, because my prayers go up to you.

Psalm 143:8 NCV

Some days there is so much to do, we don't know where to start. But Jesus can help!

Start the day right by asking Jesus to show you what needs to be done first. He can help you see what's most important. When you let Jesus lead you, He will help you care about the things He cares about. That way, you and Jesus can work together all day long. What a great day that will be!

THOUGHT OF THE DAY

Make a list of what you need to do, then pray about what to do first. It's fun to cross things off as you finish them!

PRAY TODAY

Dear God, please show me what to do each day. Thank you for always helping me. Amen.

TRUST GOD

When I am afraid, I will trust in You.

Psalm 56:3 HCSB

What can you do if you are having a problem or feel afraid? You can trust God! God wants you to talk to Him. He knows exactly what you are feeling and wants to help.

Every day you can share with God your happy times, and even your worries. He is always ready to listen. So the next time you feel afraid or don't know what to do, tell God about it. He cares about you.

THOUGHT OF THE DAY

You are very important to God—and you can trust Him with anything!

PRAY TODAY

Dear God, I'm so glad I can trust You. I love You. Amen.

YOU CAN DO IT!

As Goliath moved closer to attack, David quickly ran out to meet him.

1 Samuel 17:48 NLT

Did you know that God wants to do His work in you and through you? And God's work is always great! Even though you're just one person, He wants your life to be a full life of serving Him and His plan in the world.

The Bible is full of surprising people who changed the world. David was the smallest son in a big family, but he saved a whole army! Esther was a poor orphan who became a powerful queen. Mary came from a small town, but God chose her to be Jesus' mother. God can use anyone to do His work, and that includes you. God can use you to do great things!

THOUGHT OF THE DAY

Do your best, trust God, and watch what He does!

PRAY TODAY

Dear God, thank You that You will do great things with me! Amen.

WORKING TOGETHER

Then make me truly happy by loving each other and . . . working together.

Philippians 2:2 TLB

Everybody needs help sometimes. That's why God gave us friends and family—to help us out as we work together.

If you can't reach a book on a tall shelf, you can ask your mom if she can get it for you. And if your grandpa needs a little help picking up his glasses he dropped, you can crawl on the floor and get them for him. God knows that we all need one another.

THOUGHT OF THE DAY

Each day is so much easier when we work together!

PRAY TODAY

Dear God, I'm thankful for my family, who helps me. I want to be a great helper too! Amen.

GOD'S GREAT GOODNESS

You are wonderful. . . . you store up blessings for all who honor and trust you.

Psalm 31:19 CEV

God is so good! You are special to Him, and He loves to give you good things. He has given you a home and family, food and clothing, friends and teachers, and even more! It is good to be thankful for all of these good things, or blessings, in your life. It is even better to share God's goodness.

You can share God's goodness with others by being kind, by sharing a toy or book, or by saying thank you to your parents.

You can be happy knowing that God will continue to give you good things because He loves you so much.

THOUGHT OF THE DAY

One of the reasons God gives you good gifts is so you can share them with others.

PRAY TODAY

Dear God, thank You for all of the good things You have given me. Help me always to remember them. Amen.

DON'T WORRY, BE HAPPY!

Worry is a heavy burden, but a kind word always brings cheer.

Proverbs 12:25 CEV

What's it like when you feel worried about something? Do you have trouble sleeping or feel grouchy all day? The Bible tells us that worrying is like carrying a heavy bag around all the time. It's no fun!

But guess what? You can give that heavy bag to God! Nothing is too heavy for Him, and you'll be surprised how much lighter you feel. When you hand your worries to God, you'll be able to focus on more important things like having fun with friends and sharing His love!

THOUGHT OF THE DAY

Ask God to take your worries away, then focus your thinking on helping someone else!

PRAY TODAY

Dear God, thank You that nothing is too heavy for You to carry. Please help me give my worries to You. Amen.

DON'T GIVE UP

We can rejoice, too, when we run into problems and trials, for we know that they are good for us—they help us learn to be patient. And patience develops strength of character in us and helps us trust God more each time we use it until finally our hope and faith are strong and steady.

Romans 5:3-4 TLB

Sometimes learning something new is easy, and sometimes it requires a lot of hard work!

Did you know the Bible says that difficult things can be good for us? It's true! That's because trying very hard at something can help us learn to keep going.

The next time you are doing something hard, ask God for help. He can encourage you and remind you that He has a plan for you.

THOUGHT OF THE DAY

You'll be amazed at what you can accomplish if you trust God to help you and keep trying.

PRAY TODAY

Dear God, sometimes I just want to give up, but I know You want me to learn to keep going. Thank You for helping me keep trying. Amen.

GOD'S GIFT OF PEACE

Only God gives inward peace, and I depend on him.

Psalm 62:5 CEV

The Bible says a lot about peace. That's because it's a wonderful gift that only God can give!

The peace that God promises is something He gives you. He is in control of everything, and He wants you to live every day knowing that, both in your head and your heart. Anytime you feel afraid, you can hand Him all your worries and trust Him to take care of you. And since God's peace lives inside you, you will never lose it. What a great gift!

THOUGHT OF THE DAY

God can help you anytime and anywhere. He wants to give you peace inside your heart and mind.

PRAY TODAY

Dear God, thank You for the gift of peace. Help me feel it today! Amen.

PARENTS CAN HELP

The one who lives with integrity is righteous; his children who come after him will be happy.

Proverbs 20:7 HCSB

Your parents know a whole lot about so many things. And they want you to learn and grow into who God wants you to be! So why not ask them for their help? You can ask them to help you with almost anything. Are you trying to get better at something? Is it hard to be kind sometimes? Do you have questions about God? They would love to help you! Even if they don't know the answer to a question, they'll figure it out with you. Parents are some of God's greatest gifts!

THOUGHT OF THE DAY

Ask your parents to tell you a story about your grandparents. You might be surprised at what you'll learn!

PRAY TODAY

Dear God, please bless my parents! Thank You that they love me and want to help me grow. Amen.

NO LIE IS A GOOD LIE

Since you put away lying, Speak the truth, each one to his neighbor, because we are members of one another.

Ephesians 4:25 HCSB

It's tempting to think that a small lie doesn't matter, especially if it gets you out of trouble. But it's still unfair to the person you tell, and it could hurt someone else. The best thing to do is to always tell the truth!

The Bible tells us to "put away lying" and speak honestly. Try thinking about lying as something you put away on a high shelf so you can't even reach it. That way, you can't help but tell the truth!

THOUGHT OF THE DAY

When you tell the truth about something you've done wrong, you can ask for forgiveness and move on!

PRAY TODAY

Dear God, help me to always choose the truth and put lies somewhere I can't reach them! Amen.

LOOK FOR GOODNESS

The one who searches for what is good finds favor, but if someone looks for trouble, it will come to him.

Proverbs 11:27 HCSB

Goodness is a funny thing. It might not be obvious, but God says if you look for goodness you'll find it. You can find goodness in other people, at school, and in yourself.

Sometimes we can get distracted by things that worry us or make us upset. Looking for good things in any situation keeps your heart cheerful, because you'll find what God wants you to see. So ask God to show you good things and the ways He might be working. They are all around you!

THOUGHT OF THE DAY

Look around you. What are three good things you see right now?

PRAY TODAY

Dear God, please show me how to find goodness everywhere. Amen.

TIME WELL SPENT

But when you pray, go into your private room, shut your door, and pray to your Father who is in secret.

Matthew 6:6 HCSB

How do you grow closer to your friends? You spend time with them! You probably play together and talk about things that matter to you. If you want to get to know someone, you have to spend time together.

Don't forget that God is your friend too. He wants to spend time with you so that you can know Him better and learn to trust Him more.

Set aside time every day to talk to your very best friend. Before long, you'll start to feel as close to God as you feel to the rest of your friends!

THOUGHT OF THE DAY

Find a comfy space to use especially for talking to God. It can be your special Prayer Place!

PRAY TODAY

Dear God, help me set aside time every day to spend with You. I want for us to become better friends! Amen.

LOVE IS OUR GUIDE

Be gentle and ready to forgive; never hold grudges. Remember, the Lord forgave you, so you must forgive others. Most of all, let love guide your life.

Colossians 3:13-14 TLB

God wants us to let love guide our actions. Even when someone hurts our feelings or makes us angry, God wants us to respond in love.

How can you do this? The Bible says we should be gentle and ready to forgive, just as God forgives us. Today, think of some ways that you can let love guide you and be a blessing to everyone you meet. And the next time someone upsets you, forgive just like God forgave you!

THOUGHT OF THE DAY

Love always thinks of the feelings of others.

PRAY TODAY

Dear God, thank You for forgiving me. Please help me forgive others and let love guide me. Amen.

LET GOD WORK THROUGH YOU

"There's a youngster here with five barley loaves and a couple of fish! But what good is that with all this mob?"

John 6:8-9 TLB

Do you know the story of the loaves and fishes? Jesus needed to feed a crowd of more than 5,000 hungry people who had gathered to hear Him speak. One of Jesus' friends noticed a small boy with five pieces of bread and two fish.

What happened? A miracle! Jesus took that small bag of food and fed *all* the people. When they were finished eating, there were twelve large baskets of food left over! You may think you can't accomplish very much because you are young. But if you let God work through you, He can do incredible things in your life, too!

THOUGHT OF THE DAY

God has the power to do amazing things through you!

PRAY TODAY

Dear God, I want everything I do to honor You. Please show me what You want me to do. Amen.

GOD'S VERY OWN

Long ago, even before he made the world, God chose us to be his very own through what Christ would do for us. . . . And he did this because he wanted to!

Ephesians 1:4-5 TLB

Here's something to think about: God loves you! And He *chose* you too!

The Bible says God knew you before the world was even made, and He decided then that you would be a part of His family. He chose you and made you, just because He loves you!

God made you unique with special talents and abilities that you may not even realize you have yet. He made each one of us special: your mom and dad, sisters, brothers, and friends too.

Never forget that there is no one just like you, and God is thinking about you today!

THOUGHT OF THE DAY

You are chosen by God!

PRAY TODAY

Dear God, it makes me feel special to know that You chose me. I love You. Amen.

A HAPPY LIFE

Be satisfied with what you have. For God has said, "I will never fail you; I will never abandon you."

Hebrews 13:5 NLT

Some people think they can only have a happy life if they always get their way or if they get all the things they want. But that's not how happiness works. True happiness comes from God!

When we spend time wishing we had different things, we make ourselves unhappy. Instead, trust God to give you what you need, and enjoy the blessings He's already given you. When you trust Him, He can fill you with His joy and peace. There won't be room for anything else but happiness!

THOUGHT OF THE DAY

Look around you. What can you be happy about right now?

PRAY TODAY

Dear God, thank You for caring for me. Please help me find happiness in You. Amen.

CHOOSE COURAGE

"Be strong and courageous and do it. Do not be afraid and do not be dismayed, for the LORD God, even my God, is with you. He will not leave you or forsake you."

1 Chronicles 28:20 ESV

Many of the men and women of the Bible felt afraid when God first asked them to do something important. But then they chose to be strong and courageous. They trusted God and followed Him. And because of that, they did amazing things!

You can choose to be strong and courageous too! You may not feel that way, but God can help you. He has promised never to leave you, and God always keeps His promises. If you make the decision to trust Him, He will give you courage.

So be brave! God is by your side.

THOUGHT OF THE DAY

Try something new today. God won't let you down!

PRAY TODAY

Dear God, thank You that You'll never leave me. Please help me be strong and courageous today! Amen.

KIND THOUGHTS

A wise person is patient. He will be honored if he ignores a wrong done against him.

Proverbs 19:11 ICB

We know God wants us to forgive one another, but what does forgiveness really mean?

The Bible tells us that forgiving means giving up our anger and deciding not to hurt someone the way they hurt us. It's not always easy—especially if our feelings have been hurt badly—but ask for God's help! Tell God how you are feeling and ask Him to take your anger away.

When you truly forgive someone, you'll notice that you feel much happier. Your thoughts aren't angry anymore! Then you can get back to being a good friend.

THOUGHT OF THE DAY

Forgiveness sets everyone free from anger, especially you!

PRAY TODAY

Dear God, please take my angry thoughts away and help me forgive others quickly. Amen.

TELLING THE TRUTH

You want me to be completely truthful, so teach me wisdom.

Psalm 51:6 NCV

God wants us to tell the truth. Sometimes it seems easier to lie, but pretty soon that lie will start to bother you. You will start to feel guilty, and you might even have to tell more lies to keep the truth a secret! It's much simpler, and more loving, to tell the truth right away.

The good news is that God can help you. And when you tell the truth all the time, other people learn they can trust you and they'll want to be your friend. Telling the truth is always the best choice.

THOUGHT OF THE DAY
The truth will set you free!

PRAY TODAY
Dear God, help me to tell the truth always. Thank You for loving me no matter what! Amen.

SHOWERS OF BLESSINGS

*For the L*ORD* God is our sun and our shield. He gives us grace and glory. The L*ORD* will withhold no good thing from those who do what is right.*

Psalm 84:11 NLT

God is loving and joyful. He loves you all the time. You can trust Him always to love you.

The Bible says that God does not hold back something good from those who do what is right. He loves to shower you with blessings. Imagine a shower of rain coming down in your backyard. Water goes everywhere! That's how God's goodness is—it is everywhere!

THOUGHT OF THE DAY

Can you think of some ways God has blessed you?

PRAY TODAY

Dear God, thank You for everything You have done for me. I love You. Amen.

A GOOD CHOICE

Finally, brothers, whatever is true, whatever is honorable, whatever is just, whatever is pure, whatever is lovely, whatever is commendable, if there is any excellence, if there is anything worthy of praise, think about these things.

Philippians 4:8 ESV

God wants us to be joyful! One of the ways we can be joyful is to have a good attitude.

Sometimes not-so-good things may happen, but God helps us to choose what we think and do about those things.

The Bible tells us to think on good things, so try this: the next time it rains, be thankful because you know the rain is feeding the trees and flowers in your yard.

It's your choice, and deciding to think on the good things will help you—and others around you—to be joyful in your life.

THOUGHT OF THE DAY

Choose to have a good attitude today!

PRAY TODAY

Dear God, please help me to think on good things today. Amen.

IT'S ALL FORGOTTEN

He does not hold on to His anger forever, because He delights in faithful love.

Micah 7:18b HCSB

God promises to forgive all our sins if we just ask Him. Isn't that great news? But what's just as amazing is that God forgets all our wrongs as soon as He forgives us. It's like they never happened!

Imagine if you forgot how someone hurt your feelings as soon as you forgave him or her. You'd probably get right back to being great friends with only good memories! That's how God sees you. He doesn't hold on to past hurts. He moves on, and He's always ready to see the best in you!

THOUGHT OF THE DAY

How does it make you feel to know that God forgives your sins?

PRAY TODAY

Dear God, thank You for forgiving me so completely! Help me forgive and move on, so I don't hold on to hurt feelings either. Amen.

TOUGH FORGIVENESS

Never pay back evil with more evil. Do things in such a way that everyone can see you are honorable.

Romans 12:17 NLT

Joseph was a man in the Bible who had a tough life! His brothers sent him far away from home, and he was put in prison. But Joseph trusted God, and one day he became very powerful. He could have gotten back at his brothers, but instead he forgave them. He even helped them when they were in trouble!

God gave Joseph the strength he needed to choose forgiveness. If someone hurts you, you may want to stay angry for a while. Don't do it! Ask God to help you let go of your anger and forgive. You'll feel a lot better!

THOUGHT OF THE DAY

Is there someone you're angry with? Ask God to help you forgive them today!

PRAY TODAY

Dear God, help me to forgive people like Joseph did. I know I will feel a lot better! Amen.

JOYFUL ALL THE TIME

"Don't be sad! This is a special day for the Lord, and he will make you happy and strong."

Nehemiah 8:10 CEV

Depending on what's going on around you, you might feel happy or sad at different times during the day. We can ask God to encourage us with His love and care, especially when we are sad. He can be strong for us. This is what it means to have the joy of the Lord. It's a special gift from God that helps you feel peaceful in every situation.

When you have joy from the Lord, you are sure that God is in control, and that keeps you from getting too worried or upset. So today, ask God for joy. He would love to give it to you!

THOUGHT OF THE DAY

The joy of the Lord can be ours no matter what is going on.

PRAY TODAY

Dear God, please give me the gift of Your joy. I want to know Your peace and share it with others! Amen.

PRAY FOR OTHERS

First of all, I ask you to pray for everyone. Ask God to help and bless them all, and tell God how thankful you are for each of them.

1 Timothy 2:1 CEV

The Bible tells us that we can talk to God and pray for others. And you can talk to God about anything that's on your mind. In fact, God wants you to!

Praying for others is a great way to care for them. You can pray for people you know, like your family and friends, and you can also pray for people you've never met—even the President! After all, everyone needs God's help. So the next time you pray, think about who might need God's special care. Your prayers can bless other people in a big way.

THOUGHT OF THE DAY
Who can you pray for today? Say a prayer for them right now!

PRAY TODAY
Dear God, please be with all the people in my life and show them that You care for them! Amen.

CHEERFUL WORKERS

Work hard and cheerfully at all you do, just as though you were working for the Lord . . .

Colossians 3:23 TLB

Do you know that God cares about *how* you work? In the Bible He says to work hard, but also to be a cheerful worker!

Your chores or schoolwork may not always seem like fun, but have you ever thought about making up games when you do them? Maybe you can time yourself and see if you can finish faster than last time. Or maybe you can make up a song or a story as you do your chores. Working cheerfully at everything you do is the best way to get the job done!

THOUGHT OF THE DAY

What is one way to make your work more cheerful today?

PRAY TODAY

Dear God, thanks for giving me work to do. Please help me to be a cheerful worker. Amen.

A FOREVER HOME

But it is just as the Scriptures say, "What God has planned for people who love him is more than eyes have seen or ears have heard. It has never even entered our minds!"

1 Corinthians 2:9 CEV

Have you ever wondered about heaven? We cannot see heaven now, but we can learn some things about it from the Bible. We know it is a beautiful place God created for His children. We know that there is no pain, suffering, sickness, or even crying in heaven. We also know that it is filled with joy and light. Think of the most wonderful things you can imagine. The Bible says heaven is even better than that! One day, everyone who believes in God will have a home with Him in heaven forever!

THOUGHT OF THE DAY

Heaven is a wonderful place filled with God's glory and grace!

PRAY TODAY

Dear God, thank You for making heaven so I can have a home with You forever. Amen.

YOU CAN TRUST GOD

So we will not be afraid even if the earth shakes, or the mountains fall into the sea.

Psalm 46:2 NCV

Do you ever feel afraid? Sometimes scary things can happen, but all you have to do is remember that God is always with you. And God will always take care of you!

God is bigger than anything you might be afraid of. If you don't like noisy storms, the next time you hear thunder, say a little prayer to God, and thank Him for taking care of you. If you're afraid of the dark, remember that God is with you. No matter what, you can always trust that God is watching over you.

THOUGHT OF THE DAY

The best way to beat fear is with faith. Don't let fear win!

PRAY TODAY

Dear God, when I am feeling afraid, I will remember that You said to "fear not." Thank You for giving me peace and courage. Amen.

TALK IT OUT

Those who are sad now are happy. God will comfort them.

Matthew 5:4 ICB

Whenever you are feeling sad, talk to your parents and to God about your feelings.

Talking with your parents is helpful because they understand that the problems that seem very big to you today probably won't seem so big tomorrow.

Talking with God helps because God knows exactly how you feel, and He helps make things better.

So the next time you're sad, don't hold your feelings inside. You'll be glad you asked for help.

THOUGHT OF THE DAY

Get a journal and start writing down your questions and feelings. You'll be surprised how much it helps!

PRAY TODAY

Dear God, when I am sad, I know that I can talk to my parents and to You. Thank You for listening to me and comforting me. Amen.

PRAY ABOUT EVERYTHING

Do not worry about anything, but pray and ask God for everything you need, always giving thanks.

Philippians 4:6 NCV

Have you ever gotten a letter or a card in the mail? It's exciting! That's how God feels every time you pray. He loves to hear from you!

You don't have to wait until you need help with something to pray. Pray all the time! Tell God about your day, your family, and your friends. Tell Him what you're thinking about or tell Him something that happened today. God only wants to spend time with you, and the more you talk to Him, the more you'll find things to say. After all, He is your best friend!

THOUGHT OF THE DAY

Tell God all about your day. He can't wait to hear from you!

PRAY TODAY

Dear God, I know You want to hear from me. Help me remember to pray all through my day. Amen.

ALWAYS THERE

"Be sure of this—that I am with you always, even to the end of the world."

Matthew 28:20 TLB

Being a kid can be a lot of fun, but there are some challenges too! Learning how to do something for the first time can be hard. Meeting new people is exciting, but it can make us feel just a little nervous, too.

Just remember that you are never alone! God promised that He would always be with you—no matter what! So if you are having a tough time, talk to God about it. He is there for you whenever you need Him, every single day.

THOUGHT OF THE DAY

God is ready to help you with every problem!

PRAY TODAY

Dear God, I am so glad that You are always with me. I will talk to You whenever I feel alone or worried. Amen.

HONESTY AND KINDNESS

In every way be an example of doing good deeds. When you teach, do it with honesty and seriousness.

Titus 2:7 NCV

God wants us to be honest and kind. When honesty and kindness work together, it makes you a friend that people know they can depend on.

When we tell the truth, God wants to help us do that with love. It may take practice, but God can help! Ask God to show you how to be honest and kind today.

THOUGHT OF THE DAY

It's good to be both honest and kind at the same time, as much as possible. Be looking for ways to do that today.

PRAY TODAY

Dear God, please help me be truthful and kind, so I can show Your love to others. Amen.

A PERFECT TIME

But they that wait upon the Lord shall renew their strength; they shall mount up with wings as eagles; they shall run, and not be weary; and they shall walk, and not faint.

Isaiah 40:31 KJV

Sometimes it seems like you do a lot of waiting! You wait for Christmas or your birthday; you wait to get older so you can do the cool stuff the big kids do; you wait to go out and play or for your mom to get off the phone. All that waiting can be exhausting!

The good news is that God has a perfect plan for you and a perfect time for everything to happen. If you are patient and trust in God's timing, you can know that everything will happen just the way God wants for you!

THOUGHT OF THE DAY

Patience comes through the practice of waiting while trusting God.

PRAY TODAY

Dear God, You have the perfect time for the perfect plan for me. Help me to be patient and wait on You. Amen.

SIMPLE BUT POWERFUL

If you really keep the royal law found in Scripture, "Love your neighbor as yourself," you are doing right.

James 2:8 NIV

Have you ever heard of the Golden Rule? The Golden Rule says that we should treat others the way we want to be treated. This is how God wants us to show our love for one another.

You probably like it when people listen to you, speak kindly to you, and share with you. If you want these things from others, it is only natural that others would want the same from you.

The Golden Rule is a powerful way of showing others the love of God!

THOUGHT OF THE DAY
Show the love of God by how you treat others.

PRAY TODAY
Dear God, please help me remember to always treat others the way I want to be treated. Amen.

KEEP ON KEEPING ON

But endurance must do its complete work, so that you may be mature and complete, lacking nothing.

James 1:4 HCSB

When you keep on working and don't give up, that is called endurance. You need endurance if you want to learn to do something well, like play a sport or an instrument. But the Bible tells us that faith takes endurance too!

Each time you choose to do what God says, your faith gets a little stronger. A strong faith will help you choose God's way again and again, even when it's hard. You can also build faith-endurance by talking to God. God will help you, and He loves to hear from you! The more you follow God, the more your faith will grow.

THOUGHT OF THE DAY

Endurance takes practice. If you make a mistake, try again!

PRAY TODAY

Dear God, help me to keep on keeping on. I want to have a faith that endures, no matter what. Amen.

BE AN ENCOURAGER

You must encourage one another each day.

Hebrews 3:13 CEV

"You can do it!" "I'm on your side." "Don't give up." These are all simple things you can say to encourage someone.

How do you feel when you're trying something for the first time, or when you're doing something that is hard work? Isn't it easier to keep on trying if someone gives you encouragement? The Bible reminds us that we should encourage one another each day. So today, look around and see who needs to hear some encouraging words. Then think of something to say that will help them!

THOUGHT OF THE DAY

What can you say or do today to encourage the people you know?

PRAY TODAY

Dear God, please help me share words of encouragement with my family and friends. Amen.

A TINY SEED OF FAITH

"Truly I tell you, if you have faith as small as a mustard seed, you can say to this mountain, 'Move from here to there,' and it will move. Nothing will be impossible for you."

Matthew 17:20 NIV

Have you ever seen a mustard seed? It is tiny—almost as small as a single grain of sand. But this tiny seed can grow into a tree that is taller than a house!

Jesus told us that if we have faith even as small as a mustard seed, we can do great things. Who are we to have faith in? God, of course! He can do anything! With even a little faith in God, we can know that He will help us accomplish great things.

THOUGHT OF THE DAY

With just a little faith in God, nothing is impossible for you!

PRAY TODAY

Dear God, thank You for giving me faith. I know that with You, nothing is impossible! Amen.

PRACTICE GENTLENESS

Always be gentle with others. The Lord will soon be here.

Philippians 4:5 CEV

C an you think of someone who is loving, calm, and considerate toward others? That is called being gentle. When you are gentle with the people around you, you are treating them the way God wants you to treat them.

You can practice being gentle by always trying to say nice things, choosing not to argue, and showing kindness to those around you. If someone is upset, you can listen to what is bothering that person and let him or her know that you care. God will help you learn to be gentle if you ask Him.

THOUGHT OF THE DAY

Being gentle isn't always easy, but it makes God very glad.

PRAY TODAY

Dear God, I know You are gentle and patient with me. Help me practice gentleness with others. Amen.

GOD IS LOVE

We know how much God loves us, and we have put our trust in his love. God is love, and all who live in love live in God, and God lives in them.

1 John 4:16 NLT

There are lots of ways to describe God, but maybe the most important one is this: God is love. Everything He does comes from that truth! When He created you, He did it out of love. When He corrects you, it's because of love. When He listens to your prayers, He covers you in love.

It doesn't matter what happens, where we go, or what we do. People can disappoint us, and we can even disappoint ourselves! But God's love is always perfect, and it's always with us. You don't ever have to worry about losing God's love.

THOUGHT OF THE DAY
Everything God does is because He loves you!

PRAY TODAY
Dear God, Your love is amazing! Thank You for loving me so perfectly. Amen.

IT'S TIME TO CELEBRATE!

So rejoice in the LORD and be glad, all you who obey him! Shout for joy, all you whose hearts are pure!

Psalm 32:11 NLT

When you wake up in the morning, what is the first thing you think about? Do you think about school? Or what you'll eat for breakfast? Or your favorite new game?

Each day is a gift from God and a new opportunity to get closer to him. Remember to thank God for this brand-new day and to rejoice in His love and kindness. There's no better way to start the day!

THOUGHT OF THE DAY

God loves to see you rejoicing!

PRAY TODAY

Dear God, I am going to be glad today! Help me celebrate all the good things in my life. Amen.

IT'S NOT ABOUT STUFF!

Then Jesus said to them, "Be careful and guard against all kinds of greed. A man's life is not measured by the many things he owns."

Luke 12:15 ICB

D o you ever feel like you can't stop thinking about something you want? Sometimes we can think so much about what we want that we stop thinking about what we have or even caring about our family, friends, and the people around us.

The next time you're thinking about the things you want, say thanks for everything you have instead. Then start looking for ways to spend more time with your family, friends, and—most of all—with God!

THOUGHT OF THE DAY

Your relationship with God is the best thing you'll ever have.

PRAY TODAY

Dear God, help me want the same things You want for me. I'm so thankful to know You! Amen.

PUT GOD FIRST

"Do not have other gods besides Me."

Exodus 20:3 HCSB

One day Moses went up on a mountain, and God gave him a list called the Ten Commandments. The Ten Commandments told the people of Israel how God wanted them to live so they could be happy and blessed.

The first three commandments are all about our relationship with God. First, He wants us to love Him more than anything else. Second, we shouldn't make anything more important than God—He is the only true God! And third, we should always say God's name with love and respect.

THOUGHT OF THE DAY

Always put God first, and you will be blessed.

PRAY TODAY

Dear God, I want to always put You first in my life. Help me love and respect You. Amen.

mphasis

DAY 65

BRING OUT THE BEST

Look for the best in each other, and always do your best to bring it out.

1 Thessalonians 5:15 MSG

Friends are special gifts from God. The Bible says that friends encourage and support us.

You can be a good friend by encouraging them when they are doing something difficult and congratulating them when they do something exciting. Sometimes our friends make mistakes, but that's OK. Nobody's perfect. Be careful not to complain or criticize, and look for ways to be kind to them. When you love your friends like God asks, you bring out your best too!

THOUGHT OF THE DAY

Today, tell a friend something you like about him or her!

PRAY TODAY

Dear God, thank You for friends! Help me remember to always look for the best in others. Amen.

A PROMISE IN THE SKY

"The rainbow that I have put in the sky will be my sign to you and to every living creature on earth."

Genesis 9:12 CEV

Have you ever seen a rainbow in the sky? Did you know that every rainbow is a reminder of a promise that God made to us in the Bible?

After the flood—when Noah, his family, and the animals aboard the ark came to rest on solid ground—God made a promise to Noah. He said that there would never be a flood over the whole earth again. And as a sign of His promise, God made a beautiful rainbow in the sky.

The next time you see a rainbow, remember that when God makes a promise, He always keeps His word.

THOUGHT OF THE DAY
God's promises in the Bible are for you, too!

PRAY TODAY
Dear God, thank You for all of the promises You have made in the Bible. Amen.

MAKING NEW FRIENDS

When you're kind to others, you help yourself; when you're cruel to others, you hurt yourself.

Proverbs 11:17 MSG

Here's a secret to making new friends: be a friend first! Don't worry about getting them to like you, but instead, focus on being kind to them.

There are so many ways to be kind to someone new. Invite them to play a game with you or offer to share a snack. If they need help with something, step in! And you can always ask questions about something they're interested in. The Bible says that kindness helps everyone. Try it out and make a new friend today!

THOUGHT OF THE DAY

Be a friend to make a friend!

PRAY TODAY

Dear God, please show me ways to be kind so I can be a good friend! Amen.

SLOW DOWN!

Knowing God leads to self-control. Self-control leads to patient endurance, and patient endurance leads to godliness.

2 Peter 1:6 NLT

Are you one of those kids who tries to do everything fast, faster, or fastest? Do you sometimes do things before you stop to think about the consequences of your actions?

If that's the case, it's probably a good idea to learn to think about things before you act. And think before you speak, too. When you do, you'll learn that you can avoid lots of problems and trouble!

God doesn't want to take away all your fun. He wants to give you self-control so you can become the person He wants you to be.

THOUGHT OF THE DAY

One of the wisest things you can do is to think before you do something.

PRAY TODAY

Dear God, please help me slow down a little and think about things before I do them. Amen.

CHOOSE GOD'S WAY

"Do everything the LORD your God requires. Live the way he wants you to. Obey his orders and commands."

1 Kings 2:3a NIRV

King David gave his son Solomon some very good advice: Obey God all the time. King David knew that it's not always easy to do what God says, but it's always the right choice.

We all have to make choices. Should you share or be selfish? Should you say kind words or hurting words? Should you obey your parents or just do whatever you want? Whenever you have to make a choice, stop and think: What would Jesus do? Then do that! God will be happy you listened to Him.

THOUGHT OF THE DAY

You can choose what's right today. Just follow Jesus and obey!

PRAY TODAY

Dear God, help me make choices that make You happy. I want to follow Jesus every day. Amen.

LIVE IN PEACE

It is good and pleasant when God's people live together in peace!

Psalm 133:1 NCV

What kind of friend are you? Are you kind, thoughtful, and peaceful? Hopefully that's how you are, and your friends treat you that way too.

The Bible says it is good and pleasant when God's people live together in peace. Whether you are at school, church, or home, how you get along with others will make your life either great . . . or not.

Living in peace takes some work, but it makes everyone so much happier. So do your best to share God's love wherever you are, and peace will follow.

THOUGHT OF THE DAY

What can you do to make someone's day better?

PRAY TODAY

Dear God, thank You for my friends. Help me to always put love and peace first. Amen.

GROWING IN GRACE

But grow in the grace and knowledge of our Lord and Savior Jesus Christ. To Him be the glory both now and forever. Amen.

2 Peter 3:18 NKJV

What does it mean to "grow in grace and knowledge"? First, knowledge is how much you know about something. You can learn more about God by reading the Bible, talking with your parents, and going to Sunday school and church.

Growing in grace begins when we start to relax and trust God to take care of everything we need. And He does this just because He loves us. You can't earn God's love and grace; they are His free gifts to you!

Today, think about how you can learn something new about God and trust Him more, too.

THOUGHT OF THE DAY

To learn more about God, read your Bible every day.

PRAY TODAY

Dear God, thank You for loving me just as I am. Help me grow in knowledge and grace so I can know You better! Amen.

THE IMPORTANCE OF FAMILY

"And I will be a father to you, and you shall be sons and daughters to me, says the Lord Almighty."

2 Corinthians 6:18 ESV

Your family is a wonderful, one-of-a-kind gift from God. What a blessing it is to be loved!

Have you ever really stopped to think about how important family is? Your parents love you, of course, and so does everybody else in your family. But it doesn't stop there. You're also an important part of God's family, and He loves you more than you can imagine.

What if someone you know doesn't have a family who loves him or her? That's when we have to step in and be that person's family—the family of God!

THOUGHT OF THE DAY

What makes your family unique and special?

PRAY TODAY

Dear God, help me show my family—and Your family—that I love them by the things that I say and do. Amen.

TELL THE TRUTH

Here is your part: Tell the truth. Be fair. Live at peace with everyone.

Zechariah 8:16 TLB

It is important to tell the truth. Telling the truth means that you are being honest. God wants us to be honest with one another and with Him.

Your parents want you to tell the truth, too. Sometimes that might be hard to do, especially if you think you might get in trouble. But it is always best to let God help you be completely honest. Your parents and God love you very much and only want you to learn the right way to live.

THOUGHT OF THE DAY

Telling the truth is always the right thing to do.

PRAY TODAY

Dear God, help me to make the right choice and always tell the truth. Amen.

A GOOD THING

It is good to praise the LORD and make music to your name, O Most High.

Psalm 92:1 NIV

To "praise" means saying good things about someone. How do you like to praise God? Maybe you like to sing songs to Him or dance around your house. Maybe you like to go to church and hear a Bible story or draw a picture that shows you love God.

We can praise God with everything that we do! God loves to hear us tell Him about the good things that He does.

THOUGHT OF THE DAY

Whatever you enjoy most, do it, and have fun praising God!

PRAY TODAY

Dear God, You are so wonderful! I love You. Amen.

WHEN YOU LOOK IN THE MIRROR

Do you not know that you are the temple of God and that the Spirit of God dwells in you?

1 Corinthians 3:16 NKJV

D o you like the person you see when you look in the mirror? You should! After all, you are a very special person who is made—and loved—by God.

The Bible says that God made you in His image, and when you ask Jesus into your heart, the Spirit of God comes to live inside you! That means you look like Him on the outside and on the inside!

So the next time you look in the mirror, don't be hard on yourself. Look at yourself the way God sees you, and say out loud, "I am special and wonderful!"

THOUGHT OF THE DAY

You matter—not because of what you can do, but simply because God made you.

PRAY TODAY

Dear God, thank You for making me and loving me. Because You love me, I will feel good about myself. Amen.

A STRONG HEART

Finally, be strong in the Lord and in his mighty power.

Ephesians 6:10 NIV

God wants you to grow up to be strong and healthy. But did you know that being strong means much more than having strong muscles? God also wants you to have a strong and courageous heart. That means learning to trust Him completely.

The best way to have strength and courage is to know God. You can ask God to teach you to follow Him, trust Him, and be strong and courageous. Nothing is greater than God's power; and with Him, nothing is impossible for you!

THOUGHT OF THE DAY

There is no better exercise for building courage than reading the Bible.

PRAY TODAY

Dear God, would You help me learn to trust You? Please teach me to be strong and courageous. Amen.

KINDNESS AND RESPECT

Just as you want others to do for you, do the same for them.

Luke 6:31 HCSB

How do you think God wants you to treat people? It's simple, really. He wants you to treat others exactly the way you want to be treated: with kindness, respect, and good manners.

Respect makes a big difference because it means treating people like they matter. And they do! They are very important to God!

Kindness is also important because it shows people how much God loves them.

Always remember to show respect and kindness and use your best manners. You want others to do the same for you!

THOUGHT OF THE DAY

Before you say or do something, think about how it will make the other person feel.

PRAY TODAY

Dear God, I want to be respectful and kind to others. Help me always to do my very best to treat others the way I want to be treated. Amen.

NEW BEGINNINGS

"For I am about to do something new. See, I have already begun! Do you not see it?"

Isaiah 43:19 NLT

Spring is a time of new things growing; you look at the grass turning green and see flowers beginning to sprout. It's exciting! But God gives us new things all the time, not just in the spring. Maybe a new neighbor moves in on your street, or you meet a new friend at school.

God loves new beginnings, and He wants you to be excited about what He has planned for you! You can trust Him to know what is best for you because He loves you so much.

THOUGHT OF THE DAY

If something new is happening in your life, thank God that He will help you and be with you always.

PRAY TODAY

Dear God, help me to always remember to trust You when new things happen in my life. Amen.

BE HAPPY

I will be happy because of you; God Most High, I will sing praises to your name.

Psalm 9:2 NCV

Did you know that you can choose to be happy—even if things don't seem to be going the way you want them to? It's true!

The Bible says we can be happy because of God, not because of the things that happen to us. Happiness comes from loving God and having a thankful heart.

God never changes, and He has done so many great things for you. So make the choice to praise God and thank Him today instead of worrying about what might go wrong. With God, every day can be a happy one!

THOUGHT OF THE DAY

A thankful heart is a happy heart! What are you thankful for today?

PRAY TODAY

Dear God, thank You for everything You have done for me. I will choose to be happy today. Amen.

PATIENTLY WAITING

I waited patiently for the Lord. He turned to me and heard my cry.

Psalm 40:1 NCV

Have your parents ever told you to be patient? It's hard to wait for things we want, but we have to trust that our parents know the best time to give us things. It's the same with God!

God has big plans for you, but only He knows when those plans will happen. That means that you may have to be patient. Trust that God knows the perfect moment to reveal His great plans for you, and pray that He'll use the waiting time to prepare you for what's coming!

THOUGHT OF THE DAY

Helping others is a great way to prepare for God's plans!

PRAY TODAY

Dear God, thank You for making big plans for me. Please help me wait patiently! Amen.

A LOVE THAT LASTS FOREVER

"I am the good shepherd. The good shepherd lays down his life for the sheep."

John 10:11 NIV

Do you sometimes wonder how much Jesus loves you? Jesus loves you so much that He gave His life so that you might live forever with Him in heaven. There is nothing He wouldn't do for you, and He loves you just the way you are—with the good stuff and the not-so-good stuff. And His love lasts forever. He will never change His mind about you.

How do you receive Jesus' love? By accepting Him into your heart, spending time with Him, and getting to know Him more each day. Your life will never be the same!

THOUGHT OF THE DAY

Jesus is full of kindness and love. He will never betray you.

PRAY TODAY

Dear God, thank You for Your Son, Jesus, and for His great love for me. Amen.

BE KIND TO EVERYBODY

Don't hit back; discover beauty in everyone. If you've got it in you, get along with everybody. Don't insist on getting even; that's not for you to do. "I'll do the judging," says God. "I'll take care of it."

Romans 12:17-19 MSG

God wants you to do your best to treat everybody with kindness. That can be hard sometimes, especially when people may not be very nice to you. But that's how God wants you to treat others so they will see how much He loves them, too.

If someone says something to you that isn't very nice, try not to pay too much attention or worry about it. Just forgive that person as quickly as you can, and keep being patient and kind. God will take care of it!

THOUGHT OF THE DAY

Is there someone you know who makes it really hard to be kind? Take a minute and pray for that person.

PRAY TODAY

Dear God, please help me to be kind today. When other people upset me, help me to calm down and forgive them as quickly as I can. Amen.

LOVING CORRECTION

But don't, dear friend, resent GOD's discipline; don't sulk under his loving correction. It's the child he loves that GOD corrects; a father's delight is behind all this.

Proverbs 3:11-12 MSG

Everybody makes mistakes. Only God is perfect! But God wants the best for you, so He promises to help you learn from your mistakes. That way, you won't keep making the same ones over and over.

God wants you to know He is your loving Heavenly Father. The Bible teaches us the many ways God is our loving Father. One of the ways God shows His love for you is by caring about every detail of your life, including the choices you make. God wants to see you make good choices. To help you do that, He finds ways to teach you what you can do better next time. So rejoice in God's correction! It means He loves you very much.

THOUGHT OF THE DAY

When someone corrects you for a mistake, try saying thanks and asking what you can learn and do next time. They want to help you!

PRAY TODAY

Dear God, when I make mistakes, help me learn from Your loving correction. Amen.

YOU'RE SO VERY SPECIAL

"For I know you well and you are special to me. I know you by name."

Exodus 33:17 MSG

When God made you, He made you in a very special way. In fact, you're a wonderful, one-of-a-kind creation—a special person unlike any other.

Do you realize how important you are to God? Do you know that God's feelings for you are based on who you are—not the things you've done (either good or bad) or where you come from? And do you know that God has important things for you to do?

All these things are true, so be glad that you are you!

THOUGHT OF THE DAY

If you get frustrated with yourself, remember that God's not finished with you yet!

PRAY TODAY

Dear God, thank You for making me a special person and for loving me. Amen.

PRAY ABOUT IT!

For the eyes of the Lord are over the righteous, and his ears are open unto their prayers.

1 Peter 3:12 KJV

Is something bothering you today? Pray about it! Has something made you sad or worried? Pray about it! Do you wish you could do better in school? Pray about it! Do you struggle with self-control and wish you could do better? Then pray about it!

No matter what the situation or problem, whenever you pray about something, God hears your prayer, and He can always help. So don't worry about things or let them bother you; pray about them. God is waiting and listening!

THOUGHT OF THE DAY

Prayer always changes things!

PRAY TODAY

Dear God, thank You for loving me and for always being ready to listen when I pray. Help me remember I can talk to You about everything. Amen.

YOU MAKE A DIFFERENCE

"For the Son of Man is going to come with His angels in the glory of His Father, and then He will reward each according to what he has done."

Matthew 16:27 HCSB

Think of a time someone made you feel great. Did a friend tell you a funny story to cheer you up? Did your mom give you a hug? Even small things can make a big difference!

The world is full of people who need help. Every day you can make someone's day brighter in small ways. When you say kind things or invite someone new to play with you, you are changing that person's day for the better. You never know who might need exactly what you give them!

THOUGHT OF THE DAY

Something as small as a smile can do big things!

PRAY TODAY

Dear God, please show me how I can make a difference to someone today. Amen.

TRUST IN GOD

Trust in the Lord with all your heart; do not depend on your own understanding.

Proverbs 3:5 NLT

What do you do when you feel like something is impossible? Do you get worried? Maybe you try to figure out a way to solve the problem yourself. But what if you can't figure it out?

Guess what? Nothing is impossible for God! The Bible says that when you don't understand something or you can't solve a problem, you can always trust in God. He loves you, and He always knows what is best. Tell God your impossible problems and give Him your worries. He will help you be calm while you wait for Him to work things out.

THOUGHT OF THE DAY

What impossible thing do you need to trust God for today?

PRAY TODAY

Dear God, please help me remember that nothing is too hard for You. Amen.

SURPRISE!

The LORD your God is God of all gods and Lord of all lords. He is the great God, who is strong and wonderful.

Deuteronomy 10:17 NCV

God loves to surprise us! You can see it all through the Bible. Hannah and Abraham thought they were too old to have children, but God gave them a son. Gideon only had a few soldiers holding torches and horns, but God helped him defeat a huge army.

Stories like this show us God's strength and power. Doesn't that make you confident that God can help you, too? That's why it's important to read Bible stories! We might not see a solution, but God can do anything. So let God surprise you with what He can do for you!

THOUGHT OF THE DAY

Can you think of a time when God surprised you?

PRAY TODAY

Dear God, thank You that nothing is impossible for You! I can't wait to see how You will surprise me next. Amen.

HOW TO LOVE GOD

This is love for God: to obey his commands.

1 John 5:3 NIV

One of the best ways to tell your parents you love them is to obey them. When you do what your mom and dad ask, it shows them that you trust and respect them.

God feels the same way when you obey His commands. When He tells you what to do, it's because He cares for you. If you obey Him, you're showing that you love Him too, and you believe that He knows what's best for you. How can you obey God today?

THOUGHT OF THE DAY

How do you think God feels when you obey Him?

PRAY TODAY

Dear God, help me choose to obey You, so I can show You how much I love You. Amen.

JUST TALK TO GOD

I prayed to the Lord, and he answered me. He freed me from all my fears.

Psalm 34:4 NLT

It's normal to feel frightened sometimes. Even brave King David felt afraid! But talking to God helped him feel better.

You can talk to God too. God loves to hear what you're thinking about! Try telling God about what scares you, and ask Him to take away your fear. Remember that God loves you. He is more powerful than anything, and He wants to help you feel happy and safe. All you have to do is ask Him!

THOUGHT OF THE DAY

God will always hear your prayer.

PRAY TODAY

Dear Lord, thank You for being with me all the time, even when I feel afraid. Amen.

GOD GIVES ME STRENGTH

For I can do everything through Christ, who gives me strength.

Philippians 4:13 NLT

Can you remember learning to do something new? It takes a lot of work! When you learned to walk, you probably fell down a lot before you felt steady on your feet. When you try a new game, it takes a while to remember all the rules. Even making new friends takes practice! But God can help us do anything, because He gives us strength to keep trying. So don't give up when something seems hard. Ask God to help you, and He will make you strong.

THOUGHT OF THE DAY

All strength comes from God!

PRAY TODAY

Dear Lord, thank You for giving me strength. Please help me learn new things, even when it's hard. Amen.

LOVE BY DOING

My children, our love should not be only words and talk. Our love must be true love. And we should show that love by what we do.

1 John 3:18 ICB

I t is so good to hear the words "I love you." It makes us feel special. Another way to make someone feel special and loved is to *do* something for that person.

You could help your mom clean the house by picking up toys, be kind to someone who is sad, or draw a happy picture for a neighbor who is feeling sick.

Ask God to help you, and He will show you how to put the words "I love you" into action!

THOUGHT OF THE DAY

What are some ways you can show love to someone today?

PRAY TODAY

Dear God, please help me to love those around me today by doing something nice for them. Amen.

JUST THE WAY YOU ARE

"You're blessed when you're content with just who you are—no more, no less."

Matthew 5:5 MSG

God wants us to do our best. That means working hard at school, being kind to others, and practicing the gifts and talents He gives us. But it doesn't mean we have to be perfect.

No one is perfect! Everyone makes mistakes, and everyone needs God's help. So be kind to yourself. Try new things and remember that you're allowed to mess up. After all, mistakes help you learn! Don't compare yourself to anyone else. Everyone has unique gifts and abilities. You are exactly who God wants you to be.

THOUGHT OF THE DAY

What is something you are good at? What's something you'd like to try?

PRAY TODAY

Dear God, thank You for loving me just the way I am! Amen.

A GOOD FRIEND

You use steel to sharpen steel, and one friend sharpens another.

Proverbs 27:17 MSG

Friendship is a wonderful gift from God. You can share love and laughter and fun with your friends. But sometimes a friend might tell you something you don't want to hear.

Maybe you are thinking of doing something wrong, like breaking into line in front of another kid. Your friend might encourage you to do the right thing and wait your turn. This is how one friend sharpens another and helps us to do our best.

A good friend will tell you the truth so you can be better at what God wants you to do. That's the best kind of friend to have—and be!

THOUGHT OF THE DAY

Do your friends make you sharper? Do they encourage you to do the right thing?

PRAY TODAY

Dear God, thank You for giving me good friends who want me to be the best person I can be. Amen.

YOU CAN KNOW GOD

This is how we are sure that we have come to know Him: by keeping His commands.

1 John 2:3 HCSB

No matter how big God is, He is never too big for you to know Him. And the Bible tells us that you can be sure that you know Him when you keep His commands. That means if you talk to God and learn about Him at church and do your best every day to obey what the Bible says, then you are getting to know God.

The more time you spend with your family and friends, the closer you are to them. You can know God by making time for Him each day, just like you would a friend.

THOUGHT OF THE DAY

It is good to spend time learning about God!

PRAY TODAY

Dear God, I want to know You better every day. Help me to remember to do what You want me to do. Amen.

MADE BY GOD

I will praise You because I have been remarkably and wonderfully made.

Psalm 139:14 HCSB

You are very important to God. There is no one exactly like you! Your hair, your fingerprints, and your smile all make you special.

Since you are wonderfully made by God, you can feel happy knowing that He cares about so many details in your life. You matter to Him! God not only loves you, He likes you!

THOUGHT OF THE DAY

When you look in the mirror, praise God for what you see!

PRAY TODAY

Dear God, thank You for making me just the way I am. Thank You for loving me and making me feel special. Amen.

WHOM WILL YOU CHOOSE?

"Choose this day whom you will serve. . . . But as for me and my house, we will serve the LORD."

Joshua 24:15 ESV

The Bible tells us about a man named Joshua who had to decide whether to serve God or himself. He chose to serve God, and God was pleased.

You get to make the same kind of choice that Joshua did. Serving God means doing what God wants you to do. You can serve God by being kind to others, obeying your parents, and sharing what you have.

Joshua knew that God loved him and wanted what was best for him. That is why he chose to serve God. God also loves you and wants what is best for you. Whom will you choose to serve?

THOUGHT OF THE DAY

Choosing to serve God is always the best choice!

PRAY TODAY

Dear God, thank You for choosing to love me. Please help me choose to serve You. Amen.

PRACTICE THE TRUTH

This is what you must do: Tell the truth to each other.

Zechariah 8:16 NLT

God tells us to be honest, but sometimes it's tempting to lie. How can you resist the temptation? Practice!

Ask God to give you strength to tell the truth all the time. You can also ask Him to put a desire in your heart to be honest no matter what. The more you trust God and do what He asks, the easier it will be to choose to tell the truth. Pretty soon it will become a habit you go to right away! Your friends and family will love your honest heart, and so will God.

THOUGHT OF THE DAY

Practice telling the truth all the time this week. See how you feel!

PRAY TODAY

Dear God, please give me an honest heart. I want to tell the truth, because that's what You ask me to do! Amen.

LOVE NEVER GIVES UP

Love is kind and patient, never jealous, boastful, proud, or rude. Love isn't selfish or quick-tempered. It doesn't keep a record of wrongs that others do.

1 Corinthians 13:4-5 CEV

Love is a wonderful gift from God. God IS love! We can show others about God's love when we love others.

Love is being patient with others and showing kindness. It means you don't brag about your toys to your friends or behave rudely to your parents. Forgiving others if they have done something wrong is another way to show love. Love means seeing the good in others.

THOUGHT OF THE DAY

Love never gives up.

PRAY TODAY

Dear God, thank You for loving me so much. Please help me share Your love with everyone. Amen.

A BIG JOB

"This is my command—be strong and courageous! Do not be afraid or discouraged. For the LORD your God is with you wherever you go."

Joshua 1:9 NLT

God had a big job for Joshua. He wanted Joshua to become the leader of His people. Joshua was nervous. He was used to following his friend Moses, and he was scared to lead by himself. But God told Joshua He would always be with him.

It's normal to feel nervous when we have a big job to do. But you don't have to be afraid! God is right there with you, and He can help you do anything. So don't walk away from new things. You might miss out on something great! Just ask God, and He will give you courage.

THOUGHT OF THE DAY
When you've got a big job to do, trust God, do your best, and see what happens!

PRAY TODAY
Dear God, thank You that You're always with me, no matter what I need to do! Amen.

NO ONE LIKE YOU!

You made all the delicate, inner parts of my body and knit me together in my mother's womb.

Psalm 139:13 NLT

When God made you, He did everything right. He created you in His image with love and care, and He only made one of you. There is no one else in the world exactly like you! What a treasure you are!

You may be tempted to compare yourself to other people, but there's no point. You're unique! No one else has your story or your gifts. Your smile and your laugh make your face light up like no one else's. Trust God's work and know that you are marvelous, just the way God made you.

THOUGHT OF THE DAY

God made you special! What are some special things about you?

PRAY TODAY

Dear God, thank You for making me the way I am! Please stop me from comparing myself to anyone. Amen.

GOOD MANNERS ARE KIND

Let everyone see that you are considerate in all you do.

Philippians 4:5 NLT

Good manners are simple ways to show kindness and respect to other people. When you use good manners, you're telling others that they matter to you. And everyone wants to know they matter!

There are lots of ways to use good manners, or to "be polite." You can say "Please" and "Thank you." You can give up your seat so someone else can sit down, or resist the urge to interrupt when someone is talking. Look for ways to be polite every day. It's just one more way you can share God's love!

THOUGHT OF THE DAY

Good manners can be a way to show kindness and respect for other people.

PRAY TODAY

Dear God, please help me to remember the good manners I've learned. I want to be kind and respectful to everyone. Amen.

CELEBRATE TODAY!

This is the day that the LORD has made. Let us rejoice and be glad today!

Psalm 118:24 NCV

Every day is a reason to celebrate! Do you know why? Because God created it! He made the sun rise, the flowers bloom, and the wind blow. He made the clouds roll by or the sun shine brightly or the thunder crash. And He made today full of special opportunities just for you.

Today may not be a special day like Christmas or your birthday, but every day has something to be excited about. Who knows who you'll meet or what you'll do? Each day you can celebrate God's awesome love for you!

THOUGHT OF THE DAY

Today is a special gift. Find a way to celebrate it!

PRAY TODAY

Dear God, thank You for today. Let's celebrate it together! Amen.

TAKING CARE OF YOU

Don't you know that you are God's temple and that God's Spirit lives in you?

1 Corinthians 3:16 NCV

Your body is amazing! It's a gift God gave just to you. And when you ask God to live in your heart, it even becomes God's special home. No wonder God wants you to take good care of your body!

There are lots of ways to care for your body. You can keep it strong by eating healthy food and doing fun exercise. You can keep it safe by wearing a helmet when you ride your bike. You can keep it clean by taking baths. There are lots of ways to keep your body strong and healthy. Learn how to stay healthy and enjoy the blessings that come from having good health.

THOUGHT OF THE DAY

Name three more ways you can care for your body.

PRAY TODAY

Dear God, thank You for all the things my body can do! Please help me build habits to keep it healthy. Amen.

REMEMBER WHAT YOU HAVE

Don't set your heart on anything that is your neighbor's.

Exodus 20:17 MSG

God has given us so many wonderful gifts! Sometimes a friend gets something we really like, and we want one too. That is certainly natural. It can become a problem for us when we spend a lot of time feeling unhappy about what we don't have. But God can help!

When you feel jealous, talk to God about it. Give thanks for all the things you do have, even if they're not the newest or most expensive. Ask God to help you remember all that He has given you to enjoy and to help your heart to be happy.

THOUGHT OF THE DAY

When you're happy with what you have, you can be happy for other people, too!

PRAY TODAY

Dear God, You know the things I want and need. Help me to be happy with what You give and to trust that You know what is best for me to have. Amen.

LESSONS TO LEARN

Remember what you are taught. And listen carefully to words of knowledge.

Proverbs 23:12 ICB

You can learn a lot about life by paying attention to what your parents have to say. Sure, sometimes you may get tired of hearing the same thing over and over. But God gave you parents for a reason—He wants them to teach you what you need to know to live a great life.

You can learn things the easy way, by paying attention and taking their advice, or the hard way, by making the same mistakes over and over again until you finally learn what you should do. So do the wise thing and listen up!

THOUGHT OF THE DAY

When you have a hard decision to make, remember what your parents have taught you!

PRAY TODAY

Dear God, help me listen to my parents and learn the lessons You want me to learn. Amen.

DON'T WORRY . . . TRUST GOD

"The LORD himself will go before you. He will be with you; he will not leave you or forget you. Don't be afraid and don't worry."

Deuteronomy 31:8 NCV

D o you worry a lot about what might happen to you? If so, you aren't alone. Lots of people struggle with worry—grown-ups and kids alike.

But God tells us in the Bible—over and over—not to worry or be afraid. Why? Because God wants us to trust Him. After all, He is in control and can handle anything that happens. He also loves you and has promised to never leave you or forget about you.

So what's the point of worrying? Worry can't change anything. It just makes you unhappy. Instead, trust God and relax!

THOUGHT OF THE DAY

When you feel afraid or start to worry, sing your favorite song from church.

PRAY TODAY

Dear God, I know You don't want me to worry about anything. Help me remember to trust You and relax. Amen.

SPEAK FROM YOUR HEART

"The mouth speaks the things that are in the heart."

Matthew 12:34 ICB

The Bible says that when we talk, the words we speak show what is inside of us. If we are glad, we speak happy words. If we are upset, angry words come out of our mouths. And have you ever been so full of joy that you just had to sing a song?

The words we say let others know how we feel. That's why it's important to fill our minds and hearts with good things. Then whatever comes out of our mouths will be helpful and kind.

THOUGHT OF THE DAY

If you want to speak with love, put God's words into your heart.

PRAY TODAY

Dear God, please help me fill my heart with Your words so I can speak with love. Amen.

GOD CAN HANDLE IT

Now the God of all grace, who called you to His eternal glory in Christ Jesus, will personally restore, establish, strengthen, and support you.

1 Peter 5:10 HCSB

It's a promise that is made over and over again in the Bible: no matter what the problem is, God can handle it. We're protected by a loving Heavenly Father.

God can help you when you're sad; He can comfort you. God is right here with you, right now.

There is nothing you need that He won't do for you and no problem He can't fix. So don't worry . . . God's got it all under control!

THOUGHT OF THE DAY

God wants to take care of whatever is bothering you. So talk to Him about it!

PRAY TODAY

Dear God, I know You will take care of me. Help me not to worry when things go wrong and just to trust You. Amen.

THREE KEYS

Rejoice always, pray continually, give thanks in all circumstances; for this is God's will for you in Christ Jesus.

1 Thessalonians 5:16-18 NIV

Do you ever wonder what God wants you to do? Well, here's some good news: there are three simple keys to pleasing God. And today's verse tells you what they are!

First, always rejoice. That means be on the lookout for things to be glad about. Second, always pray. Praying is just talking to God, and you can do that wherever you are! Third, always give thanks. There are so many things to be thankful for! If you rejoice, pray, and give thanks every day, you can know you are doing just what God wants you to do!

THOUGHT OF THE DAY

Name some things you can rejoice about, pray about, and thank God for today!

PRAY TODAY

Dear God, I love You and I want to please You. Help me remember to rejoice, pray, and give thanks every day. Amen.

BEING PATIENT

Always be humble and gentle. Be patient and accept each other with love.

Ephesians 4:2 ICB

Sometimes it is hard to wait for someone who is slower than you. Other times it is hard to understand why someone can't do something that is easy for you to do.

Being patient means being willing to slow down and help someone else, even if you are in a hurry. It means being willing to explain something more than once so that another person can learn how to do it. Loving others means taking the time to be patient. Jesus is always patient with us, so we should try to be patient with others!

THOUGHT OF THE DAY

When was a time someone showed love for you by being patient?

PRAY TODAY

Dear God, please help me be patient with other people, just as You are patient with me. Amen.

SHOWING RESPECT

Treat others just as you want to be treated.

Luke 6:31 CEV

How do you feel when someone takes your things without asking? What if you give a friend a gift and he or she doesn't say thanks? Or what if someone steps on your foot and just walks away? Don't you like it better when people say please, thank you, and excuse me? The Bible tells us to treat others the way we want to be treated. When we're kind and thoughtful to others, we show them respect. Showing respect lets others know we care about them and we want to do the right thing. And it makes God happy too!

THOUGHT OF THE DAY

What are three ways you can show respect to someone this week?

PRAY TODAY

Dear God, thank You for always treating me with kindness. Help me show respect to others too. Amen.

ACTS OF LOVE

There are three things that remain—faith, hope, and love—and the greatest of these is love.

1 Corinthians 13:13 TLB

Sometimes we think of love as a feeling, but the Bible says love is an action—something we do. That means we can act in loving ways even when we may not feel like it.

How can you act in loving ways? You can wait when you'd rather rush. You can always choose to say kind words. Don't brag or act like you are better than others, and say you're sorry when you're wrong. And it's always loving to tell the truth, even if it's hard to do. Love isn't always easy, but the Bible says it's the greatest way to live!

THOUGHT OF THE DAY

What are some things you can do to show your love to others?

PRAY TODAY

Dear God, thank You for loving me. Please help me to act in ways that show Your love to others. Amen.

GOD BRINGS JOY

But let all those rejoice who put their trust in You; Let them ever shout for joy, because You defend them; Let those also who love Your name Be joyful in You.

Psalm 5:11 NKJV

The Bible is filled with stories about people with big problems. Abraham had to move away from all his friends. Moses was chased by thousands of soldiers. Queen Esther faced an angry king. David fought a giant. But do you know what all these people had in common? They trusted God, and He took care of them when they went through hard times. Because of God's love, they were each able to rejoice even when bad things happened! Joy comes from knowing that no matter what happens, God loves you and is always with you.

THOUGHT OF THE DAY

God's love for every girl and boy can turn your troubles into joy!

PRAY TODAY

Dear God, help me remember to trust You whenever I am scared or have a problem. Amen.

GOD'S LOVE LASTS

You are my God, and I will thank you. You are my God, and I will praise your greatness. Thank the Lord because he is good. His love continues forever.

Psalm 118:28-29 ICB

Do you have a toy that runs on batteries? What happens when the batteries die? Your toy stops working. Maybe you have a favorite shirt or pair of shoes. What happens if you wear them all the time? They wear out!

There's one thing you have that never stops. It doesn't even need batteries! Do you know what it is? God's love! The Bible reminds us that God's love lasts forever. It never wears out, and you can't ever use it all up. There will always be plenty of God's love.

THOUGHT OF THE DAY

Nothing is greater than God's love!

PRAY TODAY

Dear God, thank You for loving me forever. I'm so glad there is always more than enough of Your love! Amen.

HEARING GOD

"He who has ears to hear, let him hear."

Matthew 11:15 ESV

Stop and listen. What do you hear? Birds singing? People talking? Music playing? The Bible says that if we have ears, we should listen closely so we can hear God!

What do you think God's voice sounds like? It might sound like someone reading the Bible to you or telling you Bible stories at church. Maybe it sounds like your family praying. Sometimes we hear God's voice inside of us, reminding us to be kind, to do the right thing, or just to be still. Listen closely. What is God saying to you?

THOUGHT OF THE DAY

Pay attention today and see if you can hear God telling you things!

PRAY TODAY

Dear God, thank You for giving me ears to hear. Help me always listen for Your voice speaking to my heart! Amen.

GROW GOOD FRUIT

But the fruit of the Spirit is love, joy, peace, patience, kindness, goodness, faithfulness, gentleness, self-control; against such things there is no law.

Galatians 5:22-23 ESV

Where do apples, peaches, and pears come from? They all grow on trees! The Bible says that we are like trees, and the way we act is like the fruit we grow.

When we decide to follow Jesus, the Holy Spirit comes to live inside our hearts and makes us strong. He helps us make very special kinds of fruit, like love and joy. We speak kind words and show goodness to others. We are able to be patient and control our temper. Because the Spirit lives in us, He helps us grow good fruit that blesses others!

THOUGHT OF THE DAY

What kind of fruit will you grow today?

PRAY TODAY

Dear God, thank You for changing me on the inside and helping me grow the good fruit of the Spirit. Amen.

WHO ARE YOU?

And if we are God's children, then we will receive the blessings God has for us. We will receive these things from God together with Christ.

Romans 8:17 ICB

How would you answer this question: Who are you? There are lots of things you might say about who you are, but do you know what the Bible says about you? If you love Jesus, the Bible says you are God's child. That means Jesus and you are in the same family! It also means that God loves and cares for you. He always hears and answers your prayers. He watches over you and wants the best for you. Always remember that you are very special to God.

THOUGHT OF THE DAY

What are some things that are great about being in God's family?

PRAY TODAY

Dear God, I am so glad You love me enough to make me a part of Your family. Thank You for always taking care of me. Amen.

HOW TO PRAY

"So when you pray, you should pray like this: 'Our Father in heaven, we pray that your name will always be kept holy. We pray that your kingdom will come. We pray that what you want will be done, here on earth as it is in heaven.'"

Matthew 6:8-10 ICB

D o you ever wonder how to pray? One day, Jesus' friends asked Him how they should pray, so Jesus taught them a prayer we call "The Lord's Prayer." You can follow the same pattern that Jesus taught!

Begin by thanking and praising God. Ask God to make His plans here in the world happen the way they should. Then tell God what you need. Next, ask God for His forgiveness for the things you have done that are wrong. Finally, ask God to help you act the way He wants you to.

Jesus wants us to pray always. And He promises that He'll always listen!

THOUGHT OF THE DAY

I'm so glad that every day I can come to God and pray.

PRAY TODAY

Dear God, thank You for always listening to me when I pray. Help me hear what You have to say to me, too. Amen.

GOD DOES THE IMPOSSIBLE

Jesus looked at them and said, "For people this is impossible, but for God all things are possible."

Matthew 19:26 NCV

God is perfect. But people aren't! We all sin—or, disobey God—but God says we can still be part of His family and live with Him in heaven someday. How is that possible?

It's possible because God can do anything! He sent Jesus to save us from our sin. No one else could do that! So now you don't have to worry about being good enough or doing everything perfectly. All you have to do is trust that Jesus saved you, and He will make you part of His family forever!

THOUGHT OF THE DAY
Jesus makes the impossible possible!

PRAY TODAY
Dear God, Your love is amazing! Please help me trust what You can do for me. Amen.

SMILE POWER!

Smiling faces make you happy, and good news makes you feel better.

Proverbs 15:30 GNT

Did you know that you have a special power that can help people feel better? The Bible says that smiling faces and good news make you feel better. When you share a smile, a joke, or a funny story, you show you have a cheerful heart. And that makes others feel better. Maybe you can even sing one of Larry's silly songs to make a friend laugh! Look around and see who might need cheering up. Then use your "smile power" to help them feel better.

THOUGHT OF THE DAY

How you can cheer up a friend or someone in your family today?

PRAY TODAY

Dear God, thanks for giving me a cheerful heart. Help me to share some smiles today so others will feel better. Amen.

RUN FROM TEMPTATION

Run from temptations that capture young people. Always do the right thing.

2 Timothy 2:22 CEV

Have you ever seen a magnet? If you move a nail close to a magnet, the nail will be pulled toward the magnet until it is stuck. Temptation is a lot like a magnet, pulling on us to do something we shouldn't. And the closer we get to doing or saying something wrong, the harder it is to pull away. Before we know it, we are stuck and in trouble! The Bible says that the best thing to do is to "run from temptations." Sometimes getting away is the best way to stay out of trouble!

THOUGHT OF THE DAY

Remember to run toward God and away from temptations!

PRAY TODAY

Dear God, I want to please You and not give in to temptation. Help me know when it's best to run away! Amen.

LOVE AND LOYALTY

But Ruth replied, "Don't ask me to leave you and turn back. Wherever you go, I will go; wherever you live, I will live. Your people will be my people, and your God will be my God."

Ruth 1:16 NLT

God puts people into families so we can learn how to live and love. Parents, children, grandparents, and cousins all share together during fun times and hard times. When someone in a family needs help, the whole family helps. When someone in a family is happy, the whole family celebrates. In families, we learn how to love each other and how to be there for one another. That is called loyalty. God asks us to be loyal to our families and to Him. It's one of the best ways to show your love!

THOUGHT OF THE DAY

How can you show loyalty to someone in your family today?

PRAY TODAY

Dear God, thank You for my family. Help me to always be loving and loyal to them and to You. Amen.

BEING BRAVE

"The Lord saved me from a lion and a bear. He will also save me from this Philistine."

1 Samuel 17:37a ICB

As a boy, David prayed to God and trusted Him for help to be brave when he had to protect his sheep against lions and bears. Because David practiced trusting in God, he knew God could help him when he faced even bigger dangers. One day, a giant threatened to hurt Israel's army. David said he wasn't afraid to face the giant because he knew God would help him once again.

If you practice trusting God in small things every day, you won't have trouble being brave when big things come along!

THOUGHT OF THE DAY
Where do you need to ask God to help you be brave today?

PRAY TODAY
Dear God, thank You for always being with me. Please help me trust You more every day. Amen.

A SPECIAL PROMISE

"Honor your father and mother. Then you will live a long, full life in the land the Lord your God is giving you."

Exodus 20:12 NLT

God gave some special rules to Moses. We call them the Ten Commandments. One of these commandments has a special promise attached. Read the verse above and see if you can tell what it is.

The promise says that if you honor your father and mother, then God will bless you with a good life. But what does it mean to honor your parents? It means to show them respect, listen to them, and do what they say. It also means to show them love and kindness. When you do these things, your life is better, and your family is happier too!

THOUGHT OF THE DAY

What are some ways you can honor your mom and dad today?

PRAY TODAY

Dear God, thank You for my parents. Please show me how I can honor them every day. Amen.

A DREAM FOR THE FUTURE

We can make our plans, but the Lord determines our steps.

Proverbs 16:9 NLT

What do you want to be when you grow up? Do you have a special dream for your future? That's a good thing!

God has a plan that is perfect for you. His very best plans for you will come true as you follow Him.

Just trust Him and wait patiently. It's going to be great!

THOUGHT OF THE DAY

God just wants you to love Him with all your heart, and He will take care of the rest.

PRAY TODAY

Dear God, I can't wait to see what will happen in the future. Thank You for helping me. Amen.

FORGIVE THEM ANYWAY!

And whenever you stand praying, if you have anything against anyone, forgive him, so that your Father in heaven may also forgive you your wrongdoing.

Mark 11:25 HCSB

The Bible tells us how important it is to forgive people when they hurt us. But what if that person isn't sorry for what he or she has done to you? What if that person never apologizes or asks for your forgiveness? What do you do?

Forgive them anyway! When you forgive somebody else, you're actually helping yourself. How? When you forgive the other person, you get rid of the angry feelings that make you feel unhappy. Your anger hurts you. And God doesn't want you to live that way.

THOUGHT OF THE DAY
You don't need anybody else's permission to forgive. Just go ahead and do it!

PRAY TODAY
Dear God, help me to be quick to forgive all the time, every day—whether anyone asks me to or not. Amen.

THE BEST LOVE

This is what real love is: It is not our love for God; it is God's love for us. He sent his Son to . . . take away our sins.

1 John 4:10 NCV

God sure loves you a lot. In fact, the Bible tells us if we want to know what real love looks like, all we have to do is look at how God loves us. God sent His Son, Jesus, to save us. Now, because of Jesus, anyone can choose to live with God forever. No one is perfect, and we all make mistakes, but that doesn't change God's love. He loves you the way you are, now and forever.

So give thanks for God's perfect love. It's the very best love there is. And it's yours!

THOUGHT OF THE DAY

God's love is free. You don't have to earn it, and you can never lose it.

PRAY TODAY

Dear God, I love You! Thank You for showing us what love means by sending Jesus to save us. Amen.

THE GIFT OF PEACE

"Peace I leave with you; my peace I give you. I do not give to you as the world gives. Do not let your hearts be troubled and do not be afraid."

John 14:27 NIV

D o you know what it means to be peaceful? People are "at peace" when they are not afraid. That doesn't mean everything is easy for them. It just means they trust God to take care of them!

Jesus knows it's sometimes hard to feel peaceful. That's why He offers us *His* peace. His peace is perfect, and He has plenty to share. Next time you feel scared, ask Jesus to give you His gift of peace. He is always with you! He wants to comfort you and give you everything you need.

THOUGHT OF THE DAY

Why do you think God wants you to feel peaceful?

PRAY TODAY

Dear God, thank You for the gift of peace. Help me trust You more each day. Amen.

GOD'S CRAZY PLANS

"Do you think you can explain the mystery of God? Do you think you can diagram God Almighty? God is far higher than you can imagine, far deeper than you can comprehend."

Job 11:7-8 MSG

God asked people to do some pretty weird things in the Bible. He told Noah to build a huge boat in the middle of the desert! All of Noah's friends must have thought he was crazy, but Noah trusted God. When he finally finished the boat, the rain fell hard and water covered the earth. Now that boat made sense! You won't know why God does everything He does. Sometimes it might look like nothing makes sense. But remember Noah and the flood. God has a plan for everything. Trust Him completely and watch what happens!

THOUGHT OF THE DAY

God knows what He's doing, so you don't need to worry.

PRAY TODAY

Dear God, help me trust Your plan, even when it doesn't make sense to me! Amen.

BUILDING A STRONG FAITH

Those with pure hearts shall become stronger and stronger.

Job 17:9 TLB

When you run and jump and climb, your muscles get stronger. Do you know you can make your faith strong too? The Bible says that when we have pure hearts, our faith gets stronger! What can we do to make our hearts pure?

Start by reading Bible stories and memorizing verses from God's Word. Then practice what you learn: Show kindness to others, help people who are hurting, and pray for people in need. These are the kinds of things Jesus did. As you follow Him, your heart becomes more pure and your faith grows stronger and stronger!

THOUGHT OF THE DAY

What are some faith exercises you can do today?

PRAY TODAY

Dear God, please help me keep my heart pure so I can have a strong and growing faith. Amen.

USE YOUR GIFTS

This is why I remind you to keep using the gift God gave you . . .

2 Timothy 1:6 NCV

What do you like to do? Do you play an instrument or take dance classes? Maybe you draw pictures or you like to learn how things work. The special things you do are gifts from God. And He wants you to use your gifts well!

How can you use your gifts well? You can try to get better each day by practicing. If you like to sing, work hard to learn new songs. If you like to make up stories, try to learn new words to use each day. No one else has your special gifts. Be sure to use them!

THOUGHT OF THE DAY

How can you practice your gifts today?

PRAY TODAY

Dear God, thank You for the special gifts You've given me. Help me practice hard and use my gifts well. Amen.

BE GENEROUS!

"It is more blessed to give than to receive."

Acts 20:35 ESV

It's fun to get gifts or hear kind words. But it's also fun to give those things to others. In fact, it can be even better!

When you give to others, that's called being generous. God wants us to be generous with all the good gifts He's given us. How can you be generous? Some people need help to get food or clothes, so you could donate to a food bank or a shelter. Some people need you to share friendship with them. Try inviting someone new to play with your friends. You may find that giving feels even better than getting, because it means twice as much joy!

THOUGHT OF THE DAY

Be generous with kindness today. Draw a picture to give to someone special!

PRAY TODAY

Dear God, You have given me great gifts! Help me be generous and share them with others. Amen.

BE A LIGHT

"Let your light shine before others, that they may see your good deeds and glorify your Father in heaven."

Matthew 5:16 NIV

Think about what a light does. Light helps you see clearly, find the right way to go, and maybe even feel less afraid. Those are all things Jesus does, too! When you show Jesus' love to others, it's like shining a bright light for everyone. When people see that light, they'll see that you serve Jesus. And they may want to follow Him too!

Jesus depends on you to shine His light to the world. So follow His ways, be kind to others, and help people who need it. You can be Jesus' very bright light!

THOUGHT OF THE DAY

How can you shine Jesus' light at school or at home?

PRAY TODAY

Dear God, I want to be a light and show Jesus' love to everyone I meet. Please show me how I can shine bright! Amen.

IT'S WISE TO BE KIND

A kind person is doing himself a favor. But a cruel person brings trouble upon himself.

Proverbs 11:17 ICB

King Solomon was blessed with great wisdom. So when he talks about the benefits of kindness, like in the proverb above, you can be sure it's the wise choice!

Why do you think kindness is wise? Think about how you feel when you are kind to someone. How do you feel when you do something unkind? When you do something unkind, feelings get hurt and you have to apologize. It's no fun. But when you show kindness to someone else, you both feel good! So follow King Solomon's advice and choose kindness every time.

THOUGHT OF THE DAY

Choose kindness in your actions and your words.

PRAY TODAY

Dear God, please help me be wise like King Solomon, showing kindness to everyone, all the time! Amen.

JESUS WILL ALWAYS LOVE YOU

"Just as the Father has loved Me, I also have loved you. Remain in My love."

John 15:9 HCSB

The Bible makes this promise: Jesus loves you. No matter who you are. No matter what you do. No matter how you feel. Jesus loves you.

Long ago, Jesus showed His love for you by leaving heaven to come to live on earth. Jesus helped and healed people to show the power of His love. He taught His friends about God, and they wrote His words in the Bible so you can read them today! Long before you were born, Jesus loved you. And Jesus will never stop loving you for as long as you live.

THOUGHT OF THE DAY

Do you know someone who might need to know about Jesus' love? Share it with them today!

PRAY TODAY

Dear God, thank You for always loving me. Help me share Your love with others. Amen.

LISTEN UP!

My dear brothers and sisters, always be willing to listen and slow to speak.

James 1:19 NCV

Talking is fun. But so is listening! Listening is how you learn new things and make new friends.

When your parents and teachers talk to you, listen closely! They have lots of wisdom and great stories to tell. What they say may even keep you safe! And be sure to listen to your friends, too. Great friends are good at talking *and* listening.

Sometimes it's hard to wait for someone to finish before you start talking, but you can do it. Practice listening closely to what someone says before you respond. It might even change what you have to say!

THOUGHT OF THE DAY

Listen first, talk second.

PRAY TODAY

Dear God, help me remember to listen when others are talking. I want to learn new things and be a good friend! Amen.

LEARN FROM GOD

Listen carefully to wisdom; set your mind on understanding.

Proverbs 2:2 NCV

God wants you to make good choices. In order to do that, you have to listen to wisdom. And the best place to find wisdom is God!

God knows everything, and He loves everyone. You can read God's Word to learn about His wisdom. The Bible is full of good advice and great stories that show us how to live. You can also talk with God and ask Him to lead you every day. As you spend time with God and learn more about Him, you'll get to know what His wisdom looks like. Then you can make wise choices too!

THOUGHT OF THE DAY

God wants to share His wisdom with you! All you have to do is ask.

PRAY TODAY

Dear God, I want to make wise choices. Please share Your wisdom with me! Amen.

GOD HAS A PLAN

"I know what I am planning for you," says the LORD. "I have good plans for you, not plans to hurt you. I will give you hope and a good future."

Jeremiah 29:11 NCV

God is so excited about you! He made you to be very special, and He has big plans for you.

If God's making the plans, you can be sure they'll be great! He says that His plans will give you hope and a good future. God wants the very best for you. His plans might not look like your plans, but don't worry. Just keep talking to God and following His ways. And don't forget to practice all the wonderful gifts He's given you! That way, you'll be ready for everything God has in mind for you.

THOUGHT OF THE DAY

What do you want to be when you grow up?

PRAY TODAY

Dear God, please help me remember that Your plans are the best plans. Thank You for planning good things for me! Amen.

POWERFUL WORDS

Lord, help me control my tongue; help me be careful about what I say.

Psalm 141:3 NCV

Have you ever noticed that words have power? Hurtful words can make people sad or angry. But kind and helpful words can make someone feel loved, or even help them smile.

The Bible says that we need to be careful about the words we say. Sometimes when we're angry, we might say words that hurt someone's feelings. When that happens, we need to use kind words and ask for forgiveness. You can ask God to help you think before you speak. Remember that all of your words are powerful!

THOUGHT OF THE DAY

Every day we get to choose the kinds of words we want to use.

PRAY TODAY

Dear God, please help me remember that my words are important. Let me use my words to help others. Amen.

GOOD DEEDS AND GOOD HEARTS

"A good person produces good deeds from a good heart."

Luke 6:45 NLT

When you do something kind for someone, it is called a good deed. And the Bible says that when we do good deeds for others, we show that we have a good heart!

There are lots of ways to do good deeds for the people you know. You can draw a picture or make a card for a neighbor. You can help your parents or grandparents by doing your chores with a smile. You can share your toys and take turns at the playground. You can help someone who needs a friend. What are some other good deeds that will show your good heart?

THOUGHT OF THE DAY

When someone looks like they're in need, that's the time to do good deeds!

PRAY TODAY

Dear God, when my family and friends need help, please help me be kind and do what I can. Amen.

PRAISE GOD!

"The LORD is my strength and song; He has become my salvation. This is my God, and I will praise him."

Exodus 15:2 HCSB

The Bible says it is important to praise God. But how do you do that?

You praise God when you thank Him for what He has done. You praise Him when you tell Him how much you love Him. You also praise God when you sing songs about how great He is. Praising God makes God happy. But it also makes us happy, because praising God reminds us how amazing and wonderful He is. So whenever you want to feel extra joyful, just start praising God!

THOUGHT OF THE DAY

What are some ways you can praise God today?

PRAY TODAY

Dear God, You are great and mighty enough to make all the stars in the sky. Thank You for caring enough to love me! Amen.

SHARE AND GIVE

Give generously, for your gifts will return to you later.

Ecclesiastes 11:1 NLT

Jesus told us that we should be generous with people, but there are times when we don't feel much like sharing. We want to keep the nice things we have all to ourselves. But God doesn't want selfishness to rule our hearts; He wants us to share and give generously.

God doesn't want us to love our stuff more than we love people. After all, that's not a very happy way to live!

Are you blessed to have nice things? If so, don't hold back—share your blessings with others. You might be surprised how happy it will make you feel!

THOUGHT OF THE DAY
Is your room cluttered with too many toys? Give some away!

PRAY TODAY
Dear God, I want to give and share whenever I can. Please help me to be generous, kind, helpful, and grateful. Amen.

LOTS OF LAUGHTER

He will once again fill your mouth with laughter and your lips with shouts of joy.

Job 8:21 NLT

Do you ever get the giggles? What funny things make you laugh? God loves to hear His children enjoying life, laughing hard, and even singing silly songs! It's good to find things to be happy about. Playing with friends, splashing in puddles, making up dances, and jumping for joy are all ways to show that you're happy. Learn to look for the happy things in life and remember to help others be happy, too!

THOUGHT OF THE DAY
What's your favorite joke or silly song?

PRAY TODAY
Dear God, thanks for giving me so much to be happy about! Help me share a smile with everyone I see today. Amen.

A REASON TO HOPE

May the God of hope fill you with all joy and peace as you trust in him, so that you may overflow with hope by the power of the Holy Spirit.

Romans 15:13 NIV

One of the best things about loving God is that He always gives us a reason to hope—no matter what happens. What is hope? Hope means to expect something with confidence and trust. That is exactly what we are supposed to do as children of God.

God loves you and has promised to take care of you. So no matter what happens, you can expect God to take care of you. He will not let you down!

THOUGHT OF THE DAY

Trusting God is the only way to have real hope.

PRAY TODAY

Dear God, thank You for giving me hope that I can count on. Nothing is too difficult for You! Amen.

STAYING SAFE

A person without self-control is like a city with broken-down walls.

Proverbs 25:28 NLT

The Bible says that having self-control keeps you safe, but losing self-control is dangerous. Do you know why?

When we lose self-control, we sometimes say unkind words or even do things that hurt another person. Being self-controlled might mean waiting for something that you want right now or taking turns instead of always being first. Self-control helps you say words that help instead of words that hurt. It isn't always the easy way, but it is always the best way.

THOUGHT OF THE DAY

When is it hard for you to practice self-control?

PRAY TODAY

Dear God, thank You for helping me get better at self-control so I can be safe and happy. Amen.

GOD'S PERFECT LOVE

For though we have never yet seen God, when we love each other God lives in us, and his love within us grows ever stronger.

1 John 4:12 TLB

Do you know that God's perfect love lives in you? The Bible says God lives in all His children, so that they grow up in His love.

Just as God shares His love with you, He wants you to share His love with His other children, too. That's how you show you're growing up in God's perfect love. When you love other people, you show them God's love at the same time. Look around and see who might need love today. Then use kind words and deeds to let them know that God loves them, too!

THOUGHT OF THE DAY

Who can you surprise with God's love today?

PRAY TODAY

Dear God, thank You for loving me so much. Please help me share Your love with others every day. Amen.

PRAISE EVERY DAY!

I will always thank the LORD; I will never stop praising him.

Psalm 34:1 GNT

God is so good. He gives us strength and courage. He helps us feel joyful when we're sad. He has blessed us with families and good friends. He loves us all the time. So it makes sense that we should praise Him all the time!

Praise means celebrating how good God is. You can praise God by singing songs about Him, making up a dance for Him, or simply telling Him how much you love Him. You can praise Him out loud or silently in your heart. However you praise God, remember you can praise Him all day long!

THOUGHT OF THE DAY

Remember to praise God every time you pray.

PRAY TODAY

Dear God, You are amazing! Help me remember to praise You every single day. Amen.

GOOD FRIENDS

Be kind to each other, tenderhearted, forgiving one another, just as God through Christ has forgiven you.

Ephesians 4:32 NLT

Jesus showed us what it means to be a true friend. He always told the truth. He forgave His friends when they messed up. And no matter what, He was kind to everyone.

If you want to know how to be a good friend, just look at Jesus! When you play with your friends, think about what Jesus would say or do. Try to treat people they way you think Jesus would treat them. Then you'll not only be a better friend, you'll be shining Jesus' light for them to see!

THOUGHT OF THE DAY

How can you be a good friend today?

PRAY TODAY

Dear God, thank You for my friends. Please help me be a good friend like You! Amen.

GO TO GOD

Depend on the Lᴏʀᴅ and his strength. Always go to him for help.

1 Chronicles 16:11 ɪᴄʙ

God is there for you—always! You can talk to Him any time of day, whenever you need Him. That could be in the morning, after lunch, or even at nighttime when you can't go to sleep. He loves to hear from you!

Just like your mom and dad want you to come to them if you need them, God feels the same way. He loves you so much and wants to help you.

THOUGHT OF THE DAY

You can always go to God. You can depend on Him!

PRAY TODAY

Dear God, I'm so glad I can talk to You whenever I need to. Amen.

A SPECIAL FRIEND

I will praise You because I have been remarkably and wonderfully made. Your works are wonderful, and I know this very well.

Psalm 139:14 HCSB

God made each person different, with unique talents, interests, and personalities. It would be so boring if we were all exactly alike!

You may know someone who has "special needs." Maybe they look or act different, or they can't do all the things most other kids can do. Remember that no matter what, everyone needs a good friend. After all, God loves everyone just as much as He loves you! So get to know someone who is different from you today. You might make a very special friend.

THOUGHT OF THE DAY

You may not understand why someone is different from you, so ask your parents privately. And always treat everyone like you'd want to be treated!

PRAY TODAY

Dear God, thank You for making us all so special. Help me show Your love to everyone! Amen.

HOLDING GOD'S HAND

The LORD will hold your hand, and if you stumble, you still won't fall.

Psalm 37:24 CEV

Have you ever walked somewhere where it was hard to keep your balance, like a rocky seashore or a narrow curb? When you did, you probably held someone's hand so you wouldn't fall. Doesn't it feel good to know someone's there to help you?

When you pray, it's like reaching out a hand to God. He wants to hold you up! God promises that as long as you're holding on to Him—even when you stumble or feel unsteady—He is there to help you get back up. So pray for His help.

THOUGHT OF THE DAY

God's hand is always steady, no matter where you go.

PRAY TODAY

Dear God, thank You for taking my hand and holding me up if I stumble. Please help me trust You all the time! Amen.

LOVE YOU

God began doing a good work in you, and I am sure he will continue it until it is finished when Jesus Christ comes again.

Philippians 1:6 NCV

We know God wants us to be loving and kind to everyone. But there's someone you might forget: you! God wants you to love yourself, too!

You are very special to God, so He wants to make sure you treat yourself with love and respect. If you make a mistake, forgive yourself. If you're having a hard time with something, be patient with yourself. God is hard at work doing good things in and around you. You can help Him by appreciating all He made you to be!

THOUGHT OF THE DAY

If you want to love others as you love yourself, you have to love yourself!

PRAY TODAY

Dear God, help me see myself like You see me. Thank You for showing me what love looks like. Amen.

JOY THAT NEVER ENDS

A cheerful heart has a continual feast.

Proverbs 15:15 HCSB

Imagine being at a great party that never ends! The Bible says having a cheerful heart is just like that—plenty of good things and joy to last forever.

Look around and see all the wonderful gifts God has given you: family, friends, sunshine, stars, singing birds, and good food to eat. When you choose to have a cheerful heart and to think about all the loving gifts God has given to you, your joy will never end. So even when things don't go the way you want, always choose to celebrate the good things you have!

THOUGHT OF THE DAY

What are some of the wonderful gifts God has given you?

PRAY TODAY

Dear God, help me remember to rejoice in Your amazing love all the time. Amen.

HOW TO BE A FRIEND

Love each other with genuine affection, and take delight in honoring each other.

Romans 12:10 NLT

One of God's best gifts is the gift of friendship. Who are some of your friends?

The Bible reminds us to love our friends and show them honor. This means thinking about what they would like to do, sharing with them, and helping them. Good friends take turns and find ways to make each other happy. Friends cheer each other up when they are sad and celebrate with one another when they are happy. Friends who honor one another build friendships that last a long time. If you want to *have* a good friend, learn to *be* a good friend!

THOUGHT OF THE DAY

What are some good ways to honor your friends today?

PRAY TODAY

Dear God, thank You for my friends! Help me be the kind of friend I want to have. Amen.

WORD GIFTS

Say only what helps, each word a gift.

Ephesians 4:29 MSG

Have you ever thought of your words as presents? The Bible says that every word we speak is like a gift. When you choose a gift for someone, you try to find something that will make them happy. Do you choose your words the same way?

Words like "You're a good friend" or "I like you" make others feel loved. Thoughtful words like "I'm sorry" or "How can I help you?" show you care. "Please" and "Thanks" are words that show kindness. It's fun to think about giving a gift of words to people you know!

THOUGHT OF THE DAY

Who needs a "word gift" from you today?

PRAY TODAY

Dear God, please help me find kind and loving words to give to everyone I know. Amen.

PERFECT PEACE

You keep him in perfect peace whose mind is stayed on you, because he trusts in you.

Isaiah 26:3 ESV

The Bible says that if we spend our time thinking about how wonderful God is, then God will give us His perfect peace. Why is His peace perfect? Because God knows everything, and He loves you very much. So when you trust in God, you can be sure He is taking care of you, no matter what.

The best way to hold on to God's peace is to think about Him all the time. Pray every day and read your Bible, too. Fill your mind with God. Then God will fill you up with peace!

THOUGHT OF THE DAY

Trade your worries for God's perfect peace.

PRAY TODAY

Dear God, thank You for Your perfect peace. I will trust You and think about all You have done for me. Amen.

THINK FIRST!

Enthusiasm without knowledge is not good. If you act too quickly, you might make a mistake.

Proverbs 19:2 NCV

It's fun to be playful and get excited about new ideas. But sometimes we do things without thinking, and not-so-good things can happen. God encourages us to slow down sometimes and think things through.

When you think of something you want to do or a feeling you want to express, think about what could happen next. If you run outside without shoes on, what might you step on? If you shout at someone, how will they feel? When you take just a moment to think first, you can make wiser choices. You'll be safer, and everyone will have more fun!

THOUGHT OF THE DAY

Can you think of a time you acted without thinking first? What happened?

PRAY TODAY

Dear God, please help me slow down so I can make wise choices. I don't need to be in a hurry all the time! Amen.

NOTHING LEFT TO FEAR

There is no fear in love, but perfect love casts out fear.

1 John 4:18 ESV

God knows that sometimes we all feel afraid. But He also wants us to know that He can help. The Bible says that God's perfect love makes fear go away. But how?

When we fill up our minds with thoughts about how much God loves us, there isn't enough room for thoughts about being afraid. Fear has to leave when God's love shows up! Why not give it a try? The next time you feel afraid, think about God's amazing love—how big it is and how powerful it is. Thank God for loving you and see if your fearful thoughts start to disappear.

THOUGHT OF THE DAY

Name some ways God shows His wonderful love to you.

PRAY TODAY

Dear God, thank You for Your perfect love that is bigger than my fears. Amen.

SERVING OTHERS

"I tell you the truth, anything you did for even the least of my people here, you also did for me."

Matthew 25:40 NCV

Does it sometimes feel like Jesus is far away? The Bible tells us that when we help someone in need, it's like we're helping Jesus Himself! So a great way to feel closer to God is to find a way to help others.

It can be something for one person, like making a card for a sick friend, or helping your mom clean up. Or you can ask your parents or your church how to do something for a big group of people. Whatever you do, do it with a glad heart, because you are serving Jesus!

THOUGHT OF THE DAY

When you help people, you show them that Jesus loves them.

PRAY TODAY

Dear God, please show me how I can help others. I want to make You glad! Amen.

DOING GREAT THINGS TOGETHER

Two are better than one, because they get more done by working together.

Ecclesiastes 4:9 NCV

Everybody needs help sometimes. Think of how hard it would be to do everything alone. God gave us friends and family so we can help one another do great things!

How does your family help each other? Are you stuck on a hard project? Want to make something special for a birthday present? Team up with a friend or someone from your family, and whatever the job, you can do it better and have more fun when you help each other.

THOUGHT OF THE DAY

Working together makes everything better.

PRAY TODAY

Dear God, thank You for my friends and family. Show me how we can work together to do great things! Amen.

FAITH TO ACT

In the same way, faith by itself, if it is not accompanied by action, is dead.

James 2:17 NIV

If someone says they can run fast, how do you know it's true? You have to see that person actually run! It's the same with faith. The Bible tells us that just saying we trust in God is not enough. We need to *show* people that we have faith in God.

But how do we do that? We prove our faith by our actions. Being kind, sharing, and helping others are all actions that show we love God. They prove our faith is real!

THOUGHT OF THE DAY

What actions can you do today to show your faith is real?

PRAY TODAY

Dear God, please help me put my faith in action today. Amen.

HE'S GOT THE ANSWERS!

If you don't know what you're doing, pray to the Father. He loves to help.

James 1:5 MSG

Do you ever feel like you don't know what to do? You're not alone! The only one who knows everything all the time is God. So why not ask Him next time?

When you're worried about a decision, you might think you've thought of everything. Maybe you have, but you should always ask God to help you too. He can help you choose, and He might even give you an idea you hadn't thought about! God loves to help you. And since He's always working for your good, you can trust that His ideas are the best ones!

THOUGHT OF THE DAY

Start your day by praying for God's help in everything you do.

PRAY TODAY

Dear God, thank You for having all the answers! Please help me choose the things You want today. Amen.

ASK FOR WISDOM

If any of you needs wisdom, you should ask God for it. God is generous. He enjoys giving to all people, so God will give you wisdom.

James 1:5 ICB

Have you ever had a problem you couldn't figure out? Maybe you had an argument with someone, or you wanted to make a new friend. The Bible says that whenever we need "wisdom"—or don't know what to do—we can ask God and He will help us. God knows everything. No problem is too hard for Him. Take time to pray, asking God for help next time you have to make a hard decision or solve a problem. Then listen for what He wants you to know. God wants to help you out!

THOUGHT OF THE DAY

What do you need wisdom for today?

PRAY TODAY

Dear God, I don't always know what to do or say. Please give me Your wisdom every day. Amen.

WHEN TIMES ARE TOUGH

The LORD says, "I will rescue those that love me. I will protect those who trust in my name. When they call on me, I will answer; I will be with them in trouble."

Psalm 91:14-15 NLT

Some days it feels like nothing goes right. But don't give up! Hold on to God and He will help you get through anything.

Whenever you feel lost or in trouble, you can always call out to God. He's promised to stay with you always, so you can be sure He'll hear your prayer! Ask for His help and comfort, and remember that hard times don't last forever. God is with you and working out His purposes in your life. He wants to make you more like Him and closer to Him through whatever hard thing you are going through.

THOUGHT OF THE DAY

Life gets hard sometimes, but God is always there to help.

PRAY TODAY

Dear God, help me turn to You when I'm having a hard day. I know You can comfort and help me! Amen.

EVERYTHING IS POSSIBLE!

Jesus said to him . . . "Everything is possible for the one who believes."

Mark 9:23 HCSB

Nothing is too difficult for God! The Bible says everything is possible. We just need to believe that God can do it.

God can help you do whatever He has planned for you to do. He will never leave you to do it all by yourself. You can be happy knowing that if God wants you to do something, He will make it happen.

THOUGHT OF THE DAY

Start each day by putting your trust in God.

PRAY TODAY

Dear God, please help me believe You and trust You. Amen.

EACH DAY IS A GIFT

How happy are those who can live in your house, always singing your praises. How happy are those who are strong in the LORD.

Psalm 84:4-5 NLT

God wants you to have a happy, joyful life. But that doesn't mean that you'll be perfectly happy all the time. There will be some days when things will go wrong and you won't feel so great.

When that happens, you can make the choice to be strong and trust in God. If you can hold on when things aren't going so well, before you know it, things will turn around.

When you're feeling a little tired or sad, remember that each new day is a gift from God. Make it the very best day you can!

THOUGHT OF THE DAY

God is with us every day!

PRAY TODAY

Dear God, thank You for today and all of the wonderful things You have done for me. Amen.

PEACE AT ALL TIMES

Now may the LORD of peace himself give you peace at all times in every way. The LORD be with you all.

2 Thessalonians 3:16 ESV

Have you ever had a quiet feeling that everything is going to be OK? That feeling is called peace. When your parents give you a big hug, you know and trust that they love you. God gives us peace when we trust Him with any problem that we might have.

You can talk to God about anything. He always listens to you and understands. God's gift of peace can help you with whatever you are feeling. God cares about you.

THOUGHT OF THE DAY

You can have God's peace at all times!

PRAY TODAY

Dear God, I'm so glad You give me peace in every way. Thank You! Amen.

IN EVERY SITUATION

There is a right time for everything. . . . A time to cry; a time to laugh; a time to grieve; a time to dance.

Ecclesiastes 3:1, 4 TLB

Did you know that God never changes? You will grow and change. Things around you will change, and how you feel about things will change.

Some days you will feel happier than on other days, and some days you might laugh a lot or even cry. But no matter what you are feeling and no matter what is going on in your life, God is always there. His love will never change, and He wants you to know that He will always take care of you.

THOUGHT OF THE DAY

God is with you all the time, and you can trust His unchanging love.

PRAY TODAY

Dear God, thank You for being with me all the time. Please help me to remember that You will always take care of me. Amen.

IN HIS FOOTSTEPS

For you were called to this, because Christ also suffered for you, leaving you an example, so that you should follow in His steps.

1 Peter 2:21 HCSB

Did you know that Jesus has left "footprints" for you to follow? No, there aren't real footprints all over the ground. It means that Jesus showed you how to live. That's what "following Him" is all about.

What did Jesus do? Was He kind? Did He tell the truth? Did He spend time with God? Once you see the footprint, then follow Him.

THOUGHT OF THE DAY

Always ask yourself, "What would Jesus do?" Ask God to help you follow His footprints!

PRAY TODAY

Dear God, today and every day I want to follow Jesus. Help me do what He would do now and always. Amen.

START THE DAY RIGHT

Great is his faithfulness; his mercies begin afresh each morning.

Lamentations 3:23 NLT

How do you like to start your day? You might think about the breakfast you like to eat, what you'll wear, or what you and your friends are doing that day. Those are all regular parts of getting ready for the day. This verse reminds us that each day is a day when God's faithfulness and mercy are fresh and new for us to enjoy.

Try praising God for His love each morning as soon as you wake up. Thank Him while you're getting dressed and eating breakfast. Ask for His help in whatever you need for the day. Waking up with God is the best way to start your day!

THOUGHT OF THE DAY

Every morning is a new reminder of God's love.

PRAY TODAY

Dear God, I'm so thankful for every brand-new morning from You! Thank You that Your love is with me every day. Amen.

WATCHING OVER YOU

The LORD watches over you—the LORD is your shade at your right hand; the sun will not harm you by day, nor the moon by night.

Psalm 121:5-6 NIV

Even when nobody else is watching, God is. The Bible says He never sleeps, which is a good thing because that means when we are asleep or not paying attention, God is always there looking out for us.

When you go to bed tonight, think about how wonderful it is that God loves you so much that you are never out of His sight or His thoughts. That also means that you can talk to Him at any time. He is always ready to listen!

THOUGHT OF THE DAY

God is watching out for you even while you are sleeping! Isn't that amazing?

PRAY TODAY

Dear God, I know that You are everywhere and that You are always with me. Thank You for watching over me. Amen.

FOR SUCH A TIME AS THIS

"Who knows? Maybe you were made queen for just such a time as this."

Esther 4:14 MSG

Esther was a poor young woman who didn't seem very important. But one day she became queen! Soon after that, her people were in danger, and as queen, she was the only one who could convince the king to save them!

God had an important plan for Esther, but she would never have guessed it! In the same way, God has a plan for your life. You might not know what it is, but you can be sure it's very good. So trust God. His plans are even better than you can imagine!

THOUGHT OF THE DAY

You are meant to be where you are, right now. Your life is important!

PRAY TODAY

Dear God, I am so excited about Your plans for me! Please give me courage to trust You when I don't know what's coming next. Amen.

HAPPY ON THE INSIDE

I'm happy from the inside out, and from the outside in, I'm firmly formed.

Psalm 16:9 MSG

Did you know that with God's help you can have joy in almost any situation?

If you are not feeling happy, try to think about how much God loves you and you love Him. Talk to God about anything that is bothering you. Ask Him to help you remember that you can trust Him to take care of you. When you go to God for help, any worry you might be feeling will be replaced with peace and joy from God. Soon, God's joy and happiness will bubble up out of your heart so others can see it.

THOUGHT OF THE DAY

God loves you, and He made you with joy in your heart!

PRAY TODAY

Dear God, I love You and want to say thank You for loving me and giving me Your joy. Amen.

GOD COMES FIRST

"So don't worry at all about having enough food and clothing. . . . But your heavenly Father already knows perfectly well that you need them, and he will give them to you if you give him first place in your life and live as he wants you to."

Matthew 6:31-33 TLB

Did you know that God knows everything you need? He knows exactly what you need in your life, and He has promised to give it to you.

It's normal to get worried sometimes, or to want things you don't have. But don't spend time on those feelings. Remember God's promise and make sure He is always the first thing you think of. When you put God first, you'll start to see all the ways He takes care of you!

THOUGHT OF THE DAY

When you have God, you have everything you need.

PRAY TODAY

Dear God, thank You for taking care of me! Help me to put You first every day. Amen.

HEARING AND DOING

But don't just listen to God's word. You must do what it says.

James 1:22 NLT

Don't touch the hot stove!" "Look both ways before crossing the street!" "Wear your helmet when riding your bike!" What would happen if you heard these warnings, but you didn't follow them? You might end up getting hurt. God wants us to be safe, so He tells us many things in the Bible about how to live. He also reminds us that we need to *do* what He says, not just hear it. Hearing what God says to you is the first step. Doing it is the second. When you hear *and* do what God says, God honors your good choices, and your good choices honor God.

THOUGHT OF THE DAY

What can you do today that shows you have heard what God says?

PRAY TODAY

Dear God, please help me listen to what You tell me to do, and then help me do it! Amen.

THINK ABOUT GOOD THINGS

Fix your thoughts on what is true and good and right. Think about things that are pure and lovely, and dwell on the fine, good things in others. Think about all you can praise God for and be glad about.

Philippians 4:8 TLB

Did you know you can choose what you think about? And whether you think about good things or not-so-good things can make a big difference in your life! Why? Because what you think about often determines who you become and what you do.

That is why the Bible tells us to fix our thoughts on what is good and right and true. Choose wisely—what you think about matters!

THOUGHT OF THE DAY
Find good things to think about today!

PRAY TODAY
Dear God, I will choose to think on good things today. Amen.

HEALTHY AND STRONG

You were bought by God for a price. So honor God with your bodies.

1 Corinthians 6:20 NCV

How you take care of your body is really important to God. Why? Because if you make healthy choices, you will be able to accomplish all of the great things He has planned for you.

Exercise is one of the most important things you can do to keep your body healthy and strong. Do you like soccer or gymnastics? Or maybe riding a bike or playing baseball is more fun for you. Whatever it is you like to do, make time today to move around and get some exercise. It's a great way to honor God!

THOUGHT OF THE DAY

If you don't know what kind of exercise you enjoy, ask your parents to help you find something new to try.

PRAY TODAY

Dear God, I want to take good care of my body so I can honor You. Help me to make healthy choices today. Amen.

FRIENDS YOU CAN TRUST

Friends come and friends go, but a true friend sticks by you like family.

Proverbs 18:24 MSG

Friendships that last a long time have both honesty and trust. A true friend is someone you can always count on—no matter what. They always tell you the truth and always stick by you when trouble comes.

Do you want to have friends you can trust? A faithful friend is hard to find! Start by being honest and trustworthy yourself. Next, spend your time with friends who like you for who you really are. After a while, you will have friends that feel like they are a part of your family.

THOUGHT OF THE DAY

The best way to make a friend is to be one.

PRAY TODAY

Dear God, thank You for good friends I can trust. Help me to be a trustworthy person and a good friend. Amen.

GENTLE WORDS

Always be humble, gentle, and patient, accepting each other in love.

Ephesians 4:2 NCV

The Bible tells us that gentle words are helpful and loving. But sometimes, especially when we're upset, our words and our actions may not be so nice. Sometimes we may say things that are unkind or hurtful to others.

It is never a good idea to say hurtful things. It might make you feel better for a moment, but soon you will feel bad and so will the other person! The next time you're tempted to say something you shouldn't, don't. Remember that gentle words are always better than angry words!

THOUGHT OF THE DAY

God doesn't want us to spread words that hurt; He wants us to spread nice words.

PRAY TODAY

Dear God, the Bible teaches me to be gentle and kind. So I will do my best to treat other people just like I want to be treated. Amen.

GOD CAN DO ANYTHING

Jesus looked at them intently, then said, "Without God, it is utterly impossible. But with God everything is possible."

Mark 10:27 TLB

The Bible is full of stories about people who did amazing things with God's help. Noah built a boat big enough for every kind of animal in the world. Esther convinced a powerful king to save her people. Peter walked on water! Nothing is too hard for God.

The same is true today. If you are working on something hard or you don't know how to solve a big problem, ask God to help you. You might think it's impossible, but God can do anything. So don't be shy! Ask for God's help, and He might surprise you with His answer.

THOUGHT OF THE DAY

What can you ask God to help you with today?

PRAY TODAY

Dear God, thank You that You can do anything. Please help me trust You with everything, big and small! Amen.

FOLLOW THE LEADER

"Teacher, I will follow you wherever you go."

Matthew 8:19 ESV

Have you ever played "Follow the Leader"? It's a game where one person does an action while everyone else watches closely and does the very same thing. In life, Jesus is our Leader! He asks us to watch Him closely so that we know the right way to act. Any time you're not sure what to do, try thinking about what Jesus would do. Would Jesus share something with a friend? What kind of words would Jesus say to others? Then all you have to do is follow the Leader!

THOUGHT OF THE DAY

Let Jesus take the lead!

PRAY TODAY

Dear Jesus, thank You for being my Leader. Help me to follow You always. Amen.

GOD WILL MAKE THINGS RIGHT

GOD is fair and just; He corrects the misdirected, sends them in the right direction.

Psalm 25:8 MSG

God always knows what He's doing, and He never makes a mistake. On the other hand, you will probably make mistakes occasionally. We all do!

The good news is that God is full of mercy. And when we get off track, He always puts us back on the right path with love and kindness.

So don't worry. If you make a mistake and need help, just ask for His help and forgiveness. Then trust God to work out whatever needs to be made right. He's got it covered!

THOUGHT OF THE DAY

Any time you need help, just ask God. He loves you and is quick to answer.

PRAY TODAY

Dear God, when I make a mistake, thank You for giving me mercy and making things right. Amen.

WATCH OUT!

"Stay awake and pray for strength against temptation. The spirit wants to do what is right, but the body is weak."

Matthew 26:41 NCV

How do you beat temptation? Watch for it . . . and when it comes, run the other way!

Everybody is tempted to do things that are wrong. But one of the best ways to be happy (and stay that way) is to learn how to resist temptation.

You probably know what tempts you the most. The smart thing to do is to watch out for that temptation and have a plan. Ask God and your parents to help you, and when temptation comes, run the other way!

THOUGHT OF THE DAY

Think of three things you can do when you are tempted, and write them down. Now you have a plan!

PRAY TODAY

Dear God, please help me remember to run away from temptation and not give in. Amen.

LOVE YOUR ENEMY

"There is a saying, 'Love your friends and hate your enemies.' But I say: Love your enemies! Pray for those who persecute you!"

Matthew 5:43-44 TLB

Jesus said we should love our enemies. Can you imagine that? Sometimes it is hard enough to love your sister or brother, but your enemy? That seems like too much to expect!

But God knows that loving others—even your enemies—can change any situation. What do you think God could do if you loved your enemies? Maybe if you show them kindness, your enemies will become your friends. Or maybe they will want to know God. So forgive them, and show them God's love. A miracle could happen!

THOUGHT OF THE DAY

Showing love to your enemies is being like Jesus.

PRAY TODAY

Dear God, help me remember to show kindness even to those who don't treat me kindly. Amen.

A FOREVER LOVE

The unfailing love of the LORD never ends!

Lamentations 3:22 NLT

How much does God love you? So much that He sent His Son, Jesus, to earth for you! So much that because of Jesus, you can have the greatest gift of all: a forever life with God in heaven.

God's love is bigger and more powerful than anybody can imagine, but it is very real. His love for you is forever and will never fail. So tell God that you love Him too, and ask Jesus to come into your heart. When you do, He'll show you how much He loves you.

THOUGHT OF THE DAY

God loves you so much that you can trust Him with anything! Always!

PRAY TODAY

Dear God, thank You for loving me. I want to know You better and have that forever kind of love. Amen.

JUST ASK!

When doubts filled my mind, your comfort gave me renewed hope and cheer.

Psalm 94:19 NLT

When you're not sure about something, are you willing to ask questions about what you should do? Hopefully when you have a question, you're not afraid to speak up and ask.

If you've got lots of questions, the Bible promises that God has all the answers you need.

So don't ever be afraid to ask. Your parents and your teachers and your Heavenly Father want to hear your questions—and do everything they can to help you. Just ask!

THOUGHT OF THE DAY

If you're not sure whether something is right or wrong, ask your parents before you do it!

PRAY TODAY

Dear God, thank You for giving me the courage to ask questions when I need answers. Amen.

A JOYFUL HEART

A joyful heart is good medicine.

Proverbs 17:22 HCSB

God doesn't want us to spend our days moping around with frowns on our faces. Far from it! God wants you to have a joyful heart.

The Bible says that a joyful heart is like medicine—it makes you and everyone around you feel better.

God wants you to laugh and be silly! Work hard at school, and get your chores and homework done. But don't forget to spend time doing things you love with your friends and family. You were made to have fun, dance around, and laugh out loud!

THOUGHT OF THE DAY

Nothing feels as good as laughing until your belly hurts.

PRAY TODAY

Dear God, thank You for the gift of laughter. It's fun and makes everything better. Help me laugh today! Amen.

LOOKING FOR ANSWERS

So faith comes from hearing, and hearing through the word of Christ.

Romans 10:17 ESV

Faith is a gift from God, and like a plant, we can feed our faith to help it grow. How do we feed it? The Bible says that the more we listen to what God has to say, the more our faith in Him will grow.

You can listen to God by reading your favorite Bible stories and thinking about what they mean. Maybe you like the story of David and Goliath. In this story we learn that with God on our side, we can overcome all obstacles. And knowing that can help our faith grow, just like a plant.

What are some other Bible stories that you like?

THOUGHT OF THE DAY

The Bible is full of wonderful wisdom to discover!

PRAY TODAY

Dear God, thank You for giving us the Bible so we can learn more about You. Help me hear what You have to say to me. Amen.

HE IS EVERYWHERE

God did this so that men would seek him and perhaps reach out for him and find him, though he is not far from each one of us.

Acts 17:27 NIV

God is everywhere you have ever been and everywhere you will ever go. That's why you can speak to God any time you need to.

If you are afraid or discouraged, you can turn to God for strength. If you are worried, you can trust God's promises. If you are happy, you can thank Him for His gifts. And if you are excited, you can tell Him whatever great thing has happened.

God is right here with you, ready and waiting to listen. He always wants to hear from you, so why not talk to Him now?

THOUGHT OF THE DAY

You are never far away from God. If you are in trouble, ask Him for help.

PRAY TODAY

Dear God, thank You that You never leave me and that You are always listening to my thoughts and prayers. Amen.

FRIENDS WHO MAKE YOU BETTER

As iron sharpens iron, so people can improve each other.

Proverbs 27:17 NCV

A re your friends the kind of kids who encourage you to do what's right? If so, you've chosen your friends wisely. But if your friends tend to get in trouble a lot, perhaps it's time to think about making some new ones.

Whether you know it or not, you're probably going to act a lot like your friends do. That can either be a good thing or a not-so-good thing. So choose friends who make you want to be your very best self. You can do the same thing for them, too!

THOUGHT OF THE DAY

Watch and listen carefully before you decide to be a good friend with someone.

PRAY TODAY

Dear God, help me choose my friends carefully so we can help one another be what You want us to be. Amen.

THE MOST POWERFUL

I pray that you will understand the incredible greatness of God's power for us who believe him.

Ephesians 1:19 NLT

God is more powerful than anyone or anything. He created the whole world. He makes the sun rise in the morning and the stars shine at night. He is strong enough to build mountains and control oceans. And His power can make you brave!

It's hard to be brave when you feel afraid. But God is always with you, and nothing is bigger than God. All you have to do is ask for His help! Pray for God to share His power with you. Then you can face anything!

THOUGHT OF THE DAY
Even when you feel weak, God is strong!

PRAY TODAY
Dear God, I'm glad You are more powerful than anything! Help me remember to trust Your power all the time. Amen.

A GREAT REWARD

"Be glad and rejoice, because your reward is great in heaven."

Matthew 5:12 HCSB

Jesus has exciting news for us. When we invite Him to live in our hearts, He invites us to live in heaven with Him forever!

Can you imagine what Jesus' home must be like? The Bible tells us some things about heaven, like what a place of joy it will be. We will be able to walk with God, and we'll be reunited with loved ones. There will be no more sadness, pain, or fear—only love. Heaven is a beautiful, exciting promise, and there's a place just for you!

THOUGHT OF THE DAY

What do you think heaven might be like?

PRAY TODAY

Dear God, Thank You for preparing a wonderful place for me in heaven! Amen.

SAY YOU'RE SORRY

Therefore, confess your sins to one another and pray for one another, that you may be healed.

James 5:16 ESV

When you make a mistake or hurt someone's feelings, what should you do? The most important thing is to say you're sorry and ask for forgiveness as soon as you can.

Many times, the longer you wait to apologize, the harder it becomes. But admitting you were wrong and asking for forgiveness is a powerful thing. It can sometimes even help bring you closer to the person you have hurt!

So if know you have done something wrong, don't be afraid to ask for forgiveness . . . right away!

THOUGHT OF THE DAY

If you don't know what to say, just try two words: "I'm sorry."

PRAY TODAY

Dear God, when I make a mistake, help me to be quick to admit it and quick to ask for forgiveness. Amen.

GOD FORGIVES

If we tell Him our sins, He is faithful and we can depend on Him to forgive us of our sins. He will make our lives clean from all sin.

1 John 1:9 NLV

God knows that we aren't able to be perfect and that we sin. Jesus is the only One who is perfect and without sin. When Jesus came to earth, He shared the Good News that God forgives our sins.

Every time you ask God to forgive you, He does. And we can't earn His forgiveness—we have His forgiveness because of what Jesus did in dying for our sins. God forgives you for your sin, and He washes you totally clean. So when you sin, just ask for God's forgiveness. Then move forward by His side!

THOUGHT OF THE DAY

How does it feel to know God always forgives you?

PRAY TODAY

Dear God, thank You for Your love. Help me to understand that I have forgiveness and that You wash me clean. Help me to walk closer with You every day. Amen.

GOD'S LOVE STICKS AROUND

But for those who honor the LORD, his love lasts forever, and his goodness endures for all generations.

Psalm 103:17 GNT

Can you remember a time when your feelings changed? Maybe your favorite color switched to something new. Maybe you got mad at your brother or sister, or you made a new friend.

Feelings change often, but God's love never changes! You can never make God love you less because His love doesn't depend on anything you do. He loves you all the time!

When we trust God's love and let it fill our hearts, we'll feel more loving, too. Don't be surprised if you want to tell people about it. Everyone should know about God's amazing love!

THOUGHT OF THE DAY

You can honor God's love by sharing kind words and doing good deeds.

PRAY TODAY

Dear God, thank You that Your love is always the same. Help me share Your love with others. Amen.

YOU MAKE GOD HAPPY

For the LORD your God has arrived to live among you. He is a mighty savior. He will rejoice over you with great gladness. With his love, he will calm all your fears. He will exult over you by singing a happy song.

Zephaniah 3:17 NLT

When God looks at you, He smiles! He is proud when He sees you trying to make good choices, and He is excited when you learn something new. He loves to watch you make new friends and play with old ones. He is so glad when you come to Him with worries or fears, because He loves to help you. Some people think God only wants to scold us when we do something wrong, but the Bible says the opposite. God rejoices and sings happy songs about us! So praise God! You are His joy.

THOUGHT OF THE DAY

God sings happy songs about you—try singing a happy song for God.

PRAY TODAY

Dear God, thank You for caring about everything I do. I love You too! Let's sing for joy together! Amen.

GOD'S TREASURE MAP

All Scripture is inspired by God and is useful to teach us what is true.

2 Timothy 3:16 NLT

Have you ever pretended to go on a treasure hunt? Maybe you even made a treasure map! Do you know that the Bible is like a treasure map? It is filled with exciting stories about brave men and women. It contains directions on how to find treasures like joy, peace, and faith. In its pages you can discover wonderful truths like God's amazing love for you. When you have a question or a problem, the Bible always has the best answer. So start reading your Bible now—you never know what treasures you might find!

THOUGHT OF THE DAY

Ask your parents if you can have a weekly family time where you read from the Bible together and talk about what you learn.

PRAY TODAY

Dear God, thank You for giving me the treasure of Your Word. Help me to read it, believe it, and follow it every day. Amen.

SHARE THE LIGHT

A cheerful heart is good medicine, but a broken spirit saps a person's strength.

Proverbs 17:22 NLT

When you get sick, your mom or dad probably gives you medicine. Well, the Bible says that cheerfulness is like good medicine—it makes people feel better.

So how can you show cheerfulness? One way is to smile. And that can be contagious—most people will smile right back! Another way is to share kind words and deeds.

God loves it when we have a cheerful heart and share it with others. It lets them see the love and joy that God has given us.

THOUGHT OF THE DAY

Your smile can change someone's day!

PRAY TODAY

Dear God, thank You for giving me a cheerful heart and finding ways to give cheerfulness to others. Amen.

WILLING TO FORGIVE

You must make allowance for each other's faults and forgive the person who offends you. Remember, the Lord forgave you, so you must forgive others.

Colossians 3:13 NLT

The Bible tells us that when people do things that are wrong, we should forgive them. That can be a hard thing to do sometimes. The good news is that God is quick to forgive us for the mistakes we make, and remembering that helps us to forgive others.

Has somebody done something that hurt your feelings or made you angry? If you need to, talk things over with your mom or dad, and then be ready to forgive the person who upset you. If you are willing to try, God will help you do it!

THOUGHT OF THE DAY

The next time you need to forgive, think about the last time you needed forgiveness.

PRAY TODAY

Dear God, when I have trouble forgiving someone, help me remember how much You love me and how many times You have forgiven me. Amen.

A POWERFUL LIFE

God's Way is not a matter of mere talk; it's an empowered life.

1 Corinthians 4:20 MSG

What is an "empowered life"? It is living a life that is doing your best, being your best, and trusting God when bad things happen. And sometimes they do. But the great news is that with God, you will be able to live "powerfully." He will make you brave and strong. He will help you with your problems. And God will even help you find ways to help others. With God, you can do amazing things because He gives you the power to do them!

THOUGHT OF THE DAY

Always remember that with God, you are loved!

PRAY TODAY

Dear God, I want to do things Your way so I can live my life the best way possible. Thank You for helping me. Amen.

A POSITIVE CHANGE

You put on the new self, the one created according to God's likeness in righteousness and purity of the truth.

Ephesians 4:24 HCSB

Do you have some habits you wish you could break? Perhaps you've tried to change or make better choices, but you're still falling back into your old habits. If so, don't get discouraged. Instead, keep trying to be the person God wants you to be.

Even a small positive change can make a big difference. And if you trust God and keep asking for His help to change your bad habits, He will help you do it. So make a step in the right direction and keep praying. You can do it!

THOUGHT OF THE DAY

Today, make one good choice. It can change everything!

PRAY TODAY

Dear God, help me not to give up when things get hard. I want to make You happy and do what's right. Amen.

NOTHING IS TOO HARD FOR GOD

"God can do anything!"

Luke 1:37 NCV

Have you ever read the story of Moses? God did what seemed like the impossible through Moses! Moses rescued his people from a mean Egyptian king by separating the waters of a huge sea so they could walk across to the other side! Some of God's instructions must have seemed scary or strange, but God always knows what He is doing—and nothing is impossible for God!

God can do impossible things in your life, too. If you have a problem that seems too hard to solve, go to God and trust Him. He is strong enough to do anything!

THOUGHT OF THE DAY

Can you think of another Bible story where God did something that seemed impossible?

PRAY TODAY

Dear God, You are so strong and wonderful! Thank You that I can come to you, no matter how big my questions are. Amen.

GOD'S PROMISE

"I assure you: Anyone who believes has eternal life."

John 6:47 HCSB

God made a promise a long time ago: He sent His Son, Jesus, to save the world and to save you! No one has ever made a promise bigger than that.

What does it mean to know Jesus? No matter where you are, God is with you. No matter what happens or what you do, God loves you. No matter what choices you make, God never gives up on you.

Most important, God sent His Son so that you can live forever in heaven. Wow! Now that's the best gift ever.

THOUGHT OF THE DAY

God always keeps His promises!

PRAY TODAY

Dear God, thank You for all of Your promises to me, and that we will always be together. Amen.

DO IT GOD'S WAY!

"We must obey God rather than any human authority."

Acts 5:29 NLT

In the story of Joshua, the children of Israel arrived at the city of Jericho, knowing that they would finally get to go into the Promised Land. Boy, were they excited!

But when God told them what He wanted them to do, suddenly everyone had a better idea than God. In fact, they seemed to forget all the miracles God had already done for them.

Fortunately, Joshua convinced everyone to do things God's way. They marched around Jericho seven times, blew the trumpets, and shouted, and the walls fell down! Then they were really glad they did it God's way!

THOUGHT OF THE DAY

Obeying is really all about trust.

PRAY TODAY

Dear God, sometimes I have good ideas, but I know Yours are always better. Help me follow Your instructions. Amen.

DOING THE RIGHT THING

He grants a treasure of common sense to the honest. He is a shield to those who walk with integrity.

Proverbs 2:7 NLT

When you choose to do the right thing, you never have to worry about what you did or what you said. If you always tell the truth, you never have to worry about getting caught in a lie. And God promises He will shield and protect you.

It's just common sense; if you do something that you know is wrong, you'll be worried that someone will find out.

But God loves it when you make the choice to do the right thing. It may be hard in the beginning, but it's always better and safer in the end.

THOUGHT OF THE DAY

You can't go wrong if you do the right thing!

PRAY TODAY

Dear God, sometimes it's hard to make the right choice. But even when doing the right thing is hard, I know You will help me. Amen.

DON'T JUDGE!

"Don't criticize, and then you won't be criticized. For others will treat you as you treat them."

Matthew 7:1-2 TLB

The Bible says if you judge other people in a mean or critical way, the same thing will happen to you. And that is not a very fun experience!

Don't be tempted to blame, criticize, or pick on people for things like the way they look, the stuff they don't have, the place they live, or the things they do wrong. God wants you to show love to people—even if they aren't perfect. And that's a really good thing because nobody's perfect!

THOUGHT OF THE DAY

It's easy to find things wrong in other people. Instead, take the time to look for something good.

PRAY TODAY

Dear God, help me to not judge people and to always be kind. Amen.

SHARE YOUR STUFF

"It is more blessed to give than to receive."

Acts 20:35 HCSB

D o you have a closet filled up with too much stuff? If so, it might be a good time to share some of it.

Think about all the kids who could enjoy the things you don't use very much. Maybe you've outgrown some clothes or have stopped playing with some of your toys. There are always people who need help, and it makes God happy when we give to others.

Talk to your parents about some ways that you can give. It can really be a lot of fun—even better than Christmas morning!

THOUGHT OF THE DAY

Giving will always make you feel better than receiving.

PRAY TODAY

Dear God, You have given me so many things—more than I really need. Help me to give freely. Amen.

NOBODY'S PERFECT

If we confess our sins to him, he is faithful and just to forgive us and to cleanse us from every wrong.

1 John 1:9 NLT

When you make a mistake, do you get really mad at yourself . . . or maybe really, really, really mad? Hopefully not! After all, everybody makes mistakes, and nobody's perfect!

Even when you make mistakes, God loves you and forgives you, so you should love and forgive yourself too.

The next time you make a mistake, learn from it. But don't be too hard on yourself. God doesn't expect you to be perfect!

THOUGHT OF THE DAY

A mistake is something you can learn from, so you can do better next time.

PRAY TODAY

Dear God, when I make mistakes, help me to admit it and apologize if I need to. Thank You for Your forgiveness and for Your love. Amen.

NEVER STOP GROWING

So that you may walk worthy of the Lord, fully pleasing to Him, bearing fruit in every good work and growing in the knowledge of God.

Colossians 1:10 HCSB

Every day, you're learning new things and doing new things. You're growing up, and that's exciting! But do you sometimes wish you were older than you are? Maybe all grown up and on your own?

Most kids feel this way at one time or another. But you might be surprised to learn that no matter how old you get, you'll never be done growing! Even adults need to keep growing in faith, wisdom, and love.

So don't be in a hurry . . . just do your best to follow God. There are many wonderful things ahead!

THOUGHT OF THE DAY

Grown-ups still have plenty to learn . . . and so do you!

PRAY TODAY

Dear God, help me grow a little bit more every day so I can become the person You want me to be. Amen.

KINDNESS STARTS WITH YOU

Therefore, God's chosen ones, holy and loved, put on heartfelt compassion, kindness, humility, gentleness, and patience. . . .

Colossians 3:12 HCSB

If you're waiting for other people to be nice to you before you're nice to them, you've got it backward. Kindness starts with you!

You see, you can never control what other people say or do, but you *can* control your own choices. And the Bible tells us that we should never stop being kind, no matter how others treat us.

Today, look for a chance to do something nice for others. They might not be kind to you, but you might make a new friend. You'll never know unless you try!

THOUGHT OF THE DAY

Is there someone at school who you think doesn't like you? Try doing something nice for that person. He or she just might surprise you!

PRAY TODAY

Dear God, help me to be kind to others, even when it's hard. Amen.

JUST CELEBRATE!

Celebrate God all day, every day. I mean, revel in him!

Philippians 4:4 MSG

D o you expect God to do wonderful things for you today? Sometimes we forget that God is on our side and is the One who is responsible for all the good things in our lives.

Can you think of something special that has happened to you lately? Are you happy about your family, your friends, and your church? Hopefully so!

After all, God loves you, and that fact should make you very happy indeed. So think about how good God is today—and celebrate Him!

THOUGHT OF THE DAY

Heaven is going to be one big party, but we can start celebrating now!

PRAY TODAY

Dear God, help me remember that every day is a day to celebrate! Amen.

LISTEN FOR WISDOM

My child, listen to what I say and remember what I command you. Listen carefully to wisdom; set your mind on understanding.

Proverbs 2:1-2 NCV

Do you sit quietly when your parents and your teachers are talking? Have you learned how to listen respectfully—with a quiet, attentive spirit and your ears open wide? If so, you have mastered a great skill!

Listening is important for many things, and it is the very best way to learn wisdom. There is a lot you can learn from the people in your life, but you might miss it if you aren't paying attention and listening carefully. It isn't always easy, but keep practicing!

THOUGHT OF THE DAY

Listening doesn't come easily to most people. Just don't give up!

PRAY TODAY

Dear God, make me a good listener, especially when I need to learn wisdom. Amen.

GOD-TIME

I . . . wait quietly before God, for my hope is in him.

Psalm 62:5 NLT

Have you noticed how every day has lots of different times? There's morning time, bedtime, lunchtime, dinnertime, homework time, playtime, screen time, and nighttime. But have you ever heard of "God-time"? You can talk to God, praise Him, and thank Him all through the day; but it is also important to set aside some special, quiet time each day just to spend with God. Maybe that's what you're doing right now, when you're reading this book! Taking time for God each day will make all your other times even better!

THOUGHT OF THE DAY

When will you take some special time to be quiet with God today?

PRAY TODAY

Dear God, I want to know You better. Please help me remember to take time to talk and listen to You today. Amen.

STAY STRONG WITH GOD

"Be strong! Be courageous! Do not be afraid of them! For the Lord your God will be with you. He will neither fail you nor forsake you."

Deuteronomy 31:6 TLB

It's hard to do the right thing when other people do not want you to. Daniel was a young man in Bible times who wasn't afraid to do the right thing. The people around him wanted him to stop praying to God. But Daniel would not stop praying. So the people put Daniel into a den of hungry lions to punish him, but Daniel still kept praying. Then do you know what happened? God shut the lions' mouths and protected Daniel!

God says that you can be strong and filled with courage too. You can always trust God to help you do the right thing.

THOUGHT OF THE DAY

If you keep from doing wrong, God says He will keep you strong!

PRAY TODAY

Dear God, I want to be strong and courageous. Help me do the right thing, even if it's hard. Amen.

GOD'S GOOD PLANS

"I know that you can do all things. No plan of yours can be ruined."

Job 42:2 ICB

Have you ever planned to play with a friend, but then your friend got sick? Or maybe you planned to go to the park, but then it rained and you couldn't go. Our plans don't always work out because we can't control everything. But God's plans always work out because God knows everything and He can do anything! There is no power that can stop God's plans. And because He loves you, God has good plans for you and your family. Even when your plans fail, you can be sure that God's plans will always work out.

THOUGHT OF THE DAY
You can always depend on God's good plans.

PRAY TODAY
Dear God, please help me to remember that You have wonderful plans for me. Thank You for loving me so much! Amen.

BE NICE TO YOUR FAMILY

If a kingdom is divided against itself, that kingdom cannot stand. If a house is divided against itself, that house will not be able to stand.

Mark 3:24-25 NASB

What is a divided house? It's a family that doesn't stick together and work as a team, especially when things go wrong.

God made families because we all need a safe place that feels like home, where we are loved for who we are. We all need to feel like we belong and that someone will stick by us, no matter what.

If your family has a hard time sticking together, ask God to show you how to help change that. And if you have a great team at home, thank Him for the wonderful family you have!

THOUGHT OF THE DAY

Every family gets on each other's nerves sometimes. When that happens, don't say words that are unkind. Instead, take a break!

PRAY TODAY

Dear God, thank You for my family. Help me always remember to treat them with love and respect. Amen.

HOLD ON TO THE TRUTH

Don't ever forget kindness and truth. Wear them like a necklace. Write them on your heart as if on a tablet.

Proverbs 3:3 NCV

Telling the truth isn't always easy. Sometimes you might be afraid you'll get into trouble, so a lie seems a lot easier.

But God loves truth. All through the Bible He tells us that being truthful is the best way, and Jesus even says that He is the Truth! So if we want to walk closely with God and know His will, we have to tell the truth. It may not feel easy, but you can ask for God's help. He will give you courage to tell the truth, and you will feel so much better!

THOUGHT OF THE DAY

Can you think of a time you were glad you told the truth?

PRAY TODAY

Dear God, I know telling the truth is best, but it can be hard. Please make me brave and truthful all the time. Amen.

GOOD HABITS

I can do anything I want to if Christ has not said no, but some of these things aren't good for me.

1 Corinthians 6:12 TLB

Anything you do regularly is a habit. Good habits help us grow healthy and become who God wants us to be. But bad habits can keep us from living the full life God wants for us.

Take a look at what you do each day. Brushing your teeth, going to bed on time, and reading your Bible are all very good habits because they build your body, mind, and spirit. Can you think of some habits that are less helpful? Ask your mom or dad for help, and you'll be breaking bad habits in no time!

THOUGHT OF THE DAY

To start a new habit, do it at the same time every day. In three weeks, it should stick!

PRAY TODAY

Dear God, please help me break bad habits and make good habits. I want to be all You made me to be! Amen.

LEND A HAND

Never walk away from someone who deserves help; your hand is God's hand for that person.

Proverbs 3:27 MSG

Jesus told a story about a man who saw a person injured on the side of the road. The man went over right away and did what he could to help. Because of his kindness, the injured person's life was saved!

There are people in your school or church or neighborhood who need help. Ask God to show you who they are and how you can make a difference. The man on the road used what he had to help the person in front of him. What can you do to help others?

THOUGHT OF THE DAY

Think of some creative ways to help someone in your community.

PRAY TODAY

Dear God, please show me people who need my help. I want to use my gifts to serve others. Amen.

TELL IT LIKE IT IS

I have no greater joy than this: to hear that my children are walking in the truth.

3 John 1:4 HCSB

Have you ever told a fib to try to get out of trouble? If so, you probably know that fibs can quickly get out of control. In fact, you might have to keep telling lie after lie just to keep from getting caught!

But the Bible says that God loves it when we "walk in truth." It is always best to be completely honest. Even if you think you are going to get in trouble, it is better to face the consequences of your mistake rather than make it worse by lying.

The best thing to do is to always tell it like it is!

THOUGHT OF THE DAY

Truth is always your friend.

PRAY TODAY

Dear God, help me not to give in to the temptation to exaggerate, fib, or lie my way out of a problem. The truth is always best. Amen.

GIVE IT TO GOD

Since God assured us, "I'll never let you down, never walk off and leave you," we can boldly quote, God is there, ready to help; I'm fearless no matter what. Who or what can get to me?

Hebrews 13:5-6 MSG

D o you have a problem that you can't figure out? There is only one thing you need to do: turn that problem over to God. He can handle it!

God has a way of solving our problems for us if we let Him—nothing is impossible for Him! If you're worried or discouraged, pray about it. Ask your parents and friends to pray about it too. Then give it to God and stop worrying because no problem is too big for Him—not even yours!

THOUGHT OF THE DAY

If something is bothering you, write a note to God and ask for His help.

PRAY TODAY

Dear God, I am so glad there is no problem that is too big for You. Thank You for helping me with mine. Amen.

A GREAT LIFE

I came that they may have and enjoy life, and have it in abundance (to the full, till it overflows).

John 10:10 AMP

Jesus tells us He wants us to enjoy a full life. That's great news! It means He has wonderful plans for you.

You may not know what His plans are yet, but start by living a full life today! Love your family and friends the best you can. Look for ways to show others what it feels like to be loved by God. Find a way to be joyful in every task—even your chores and homework! If your life overflows with joy, you'll be ready for all God has planned for you.

THOUGHT OF THE DAY

How can you find joy in everyday things?

PRAY TODAY

Dear God, I know You want me to have a full life. Help me find joy everywhere! Amen.

ALWAYS THANKFUL

Give thanks in everything, for this is God's will for you in Christ Jesus.

1 Thessalonians 5:18 HCSB

Sometimes you may not feel very thankful. But when you give thanks in everything, you start to find good everywhere. And that means you start to find *God* everywhere!

Is it raining outside? Give thanks that God is giving the flowers plenty to drink. Your friend can't come over today? Give thanks to God for the time to invent a brand-new game to play. There's a way to be thankful in every situation. When you look closely, God can show you His love in surprising places!

THOUGHT OF THE DAY

What can you give thanks for today?

PRAY TODAY

Dear God, thank You for everything! Help me find things to be thankful for all day. Amen.

BEST FRIEND FOREVER

And I am convinced that nothing can ever separate us from his love. . . . Whether we are high above the sky or in the deepest ocean, nothing in all creation will ever be able to separate us from the love of God that is revealed in Christ Jesus our Lord.

Romans 8:38-39 NLT

Do you know how much God loves you? He loves you wherever you are, however you feel, and whatever happens to you. God will never stop loving you. He is your best friend forever!

You can get an idea of God's love by reading the story of Jesus in the Bible. Jesus left His perfect home in heaven to be with you and me. And because He died for us, we get to share His perfect home forever if we ask Him. So if you haven't asked God to be your friend yet, why not do it today?

THOUGHT OF THE DAY

The Bible is full of stories of God's love. Can you think of one?

PRAY TODAY

Dear God, thank You for loving me so much and being my best friend forever! Amen.

BE A FRIEND!

Greater love has no one than this, that someone lay down his life for his friends.

John 15:13 ESV

Laura and Junior have been friends for a long time. They know that friendship can be a wonderful thing. The very best friends always have your back and stick with you no matter what happens.

That's why it's good to know how to make and to keep good friends. How do you do it? Remember to treat people the way you want to be treated. Be kind. Share. Say nice things. Be helpful. Pay attention to how they feel. When you do, you'll see that making friends isn't hard at all!

THOUGHT OF THE DAY

What makes your friends happy? Pick two kind things to do for friends this week.

PRAY TODAY

Dear God, help me to be a good friend to others and do whatever I can to help them. Amen.

LOOK AT THE GOOD

*I said to myself, "Relax and rest. G*OD* has showered you with blessings."*

Psalm 116:7 MSG

When things don't go the way you want, it's easy to feel upset. But here's a way to feel better: look at the good!

Everything God does is good. You can think about your family and friends. You can remember the times God has comforted you and helped you. And you can imagine the amazing plans He has for you. When you start thinking of all the good things in your life, bad things don't seem so big after all. So the next time you have a not-so-great day, look at the good! God's goodness makes everything better.

THOUGHT OF THE DAY

Good things from God are called "blessings." Try to count your blessings—you may have more than you think!

PRAY TODAY

Dear God, You've given me so many blessings! Help me remember them when I'm having a hard day. Amen.

HOW TO TREAT OTHERS

For if you refuse to act kindly, you can hardly expect to be treated kindly. Kind mercy wins over harsh judgment every time.

James 2:12–13 MSG

We all like to be treated with kindness—even a warm smile can make the day feel happier. The trick is to pay attention to how you treat others. If you are kind and thoughtful, treat people with respect, and forgive others when they make a mistake, you can be sure people will be kind to you too.

THOUGHT OF THE DAY

Before you say or do anything, make sure it is full of kindness.

PRAY TODAY

Dear God, I want to be helpful and kind. Please show me the best way to treat others. Amen.

DO NOT WITHHOLD GOOD

Do not withhold good from those who deserve it when it's in your power to help them.

Proverbs 3:27 NLT

You and your family may be blessed and may have all you need. But others in your community might need help. They may be hungry or sick or sad.

The Bible says we should not withhold help when we are able to give it. How can you help those around you? Maybe you can collect and donate food or clothes or blankets. It's not just about giving stuff—sometimes a smile and a kind word can make a big difference in some-one's day.

Today, and every day, let God show you how you can make a difference in the world around you.

THOUGHT OF THE DAY

You don't have to be a grown-up to help others!

PRAY TODAY

Dear God, thank You for all of the wonderful things You have given me. Help me see the people around me whom I can help. Amen.

ENCOURAGING WORDS

Say only what is good and helpful to those you are talking to, and what will give them a blessing.

Ephesians 4:29 TLB

Everyone needs to be encouraged once in a while! Can you think of a time when someone made you feel better with kind words? What did that person say?

Sometimes, one of the best ways to help others is by saying nice, helpful, and comforting things. For example, you can tell them that you care about them or remind them that God loves them very much.

The next time you want to help a friend who needs encouragement, speak up! You will be glad you did.

THOUGHT OF THE DAY

A little encouragement goes a long way!

PRAY TODAY

Dear God, please give me good and helpful words when someone needs encouragement. Amen.

GOD'S GOOD PROMISES

Surely goodness and mercy shall follow me all the days of my life, and I shall dwell in the house of the Lord forever.

Psalm 23:6 ESV

The Bible is filled with wonderful promises. In the verse above, David reminds us of God's promise that goodness and mercy will be with us every day and that we will live with God forever! God never breaks His promises. That means that even if we do not feel like good things are happening, we can be sure that God is still good. Why not practice looking for something good every single day? When things aren't going the way you like, think about how God is with you even then. God is good and His promises are always true!

THOUGHT OF THE DAY

Can you think of at least three good things about today?

PRAY TODAY

Dear God, thank You for your good promises to me and to my family. I love You. Amen.

START YOUR DAY WITH JOY

"You will live in joy and peace."

Isaiah 55:12 NLT

When you first wake up in the morning and you are all snug in your bed, what is the first thing you do? Maybe you yawn and stretch and think about your day. God makes every day special, so we should feel happy about our day—even before it begins.

The Bible says that we "will live in joy and peace." That sounds wonderful! You can feel joyful and peaceful by talking to God before you even get out of bed. Thank Him for watching over your family through the night. Thank Him for the birds you may hear outside your window. Just a few minutes of talking with God can help you have a great day.

THOUGHT OF THE DAY
The joy of the Lord is your strength!

PRAY TODAY
Dear God, thank You for giving me joy and peace to begin my day. Amen.

SMALL CHOICES, BIG HERO

"This is what the Lord All-Powerful says: 'Do what is right and true. Be kind and merciful to each other.'"

Zechariah 7:9 NCV

You may have heard someone called a "hero" because he or she did something big and brave. But you can be a hero by doing small things, too!

God tells us that little things can help others in a big way. You can show kindness by sharing with others and speaking nice words. You can show mercy by forgiving a friend quickly, or caring for someone who is sick. These things may not seem very big, but to the person who receives your kindness and mercy, you'll be a hero!

THOUGHT OF THE DAY

What are some ways you can be kind and merciful today?

PRAY TODAY

Dear God, please help me show Your kindness and mercy to everyone I meet. Amen.

RELUCTANT ROYALTY

"Who knows if perhaps you were made queen for just such a time as this?"

Esther 4:14 NLT

Have you ever wanted to be a king? Many kids dream of living in a castle and wearing a crown. But the Bible tells about a girl named Esther who didn't want that at all.

Esther didn't care one bit about being a queen, but God had other plans. He needed Esther to become queen so that she could save her people. Fortunately, Esther said yes. She bravely obeyed, and God blessed her.

You can trust God and obey Him. He will guide you and take care of you—He has great plans for you!

THOUGHT OF THE DAY

Whatever God wants you to do, He will help you do it!

PRAY TODAY

Dear God, I don't know what You have planned for me, but help me to be ready and brave when it is time. Amen.

YOU CAN ALWAYS TRUST GOD

Commit everything you do to the Lord. Trust him, and he will help you.

Psalm 37:5 NLT

Sometimes people will let you down, but God never will. You can always trust God because He will never leave you, not even for a moment, and He will never tell you a lie.

The Bible makes many promises, and God always keeps every single one of them. He never breaks His word, and He is always there to help you. So remember this: no matter where you are or what you're doing, the Lord is with you, and He's on your side. Always!

THOUGHT OF THE DAY

Even when you don't understand what God's doing, you can be sure that He loves you very much!

PRAY TODAY

Dear God, thank You for always loving me and always keeping Your promises to me. Amen.

KIND AND COURTEOUS

Remind them . . . to speak evil of no one, to avoid quarreling, to be gentle, and to show perfect courtesy toward all people.

Titus 3:1-2 ESV

Did you know that one of the simplest ways to love others is to show them courtesy? That simply means being polite and using good manners.

Wherever you go, you will have an opportunity to meet and talk to people. Using good manners—like saying "Please" and "Thank you," paying attention when someone speaks to you, and allowing others to go first—is a simple way you can show kindness and respect.

If you are kind and thoughtful, people will see the love of God in you.

THOUGHT OF THE DAY

The best manners are really about putting others first.

PRAY TODAY

Dear God, You can use something as simple as my manners to reach people. Please help me to do my best. Amen.

JESUS LOVES YOU!

And so we know and rely on the love God has for us. God is love. Whoever lives in love lives in God, and God in them.

1 John 4:16 NIV

Have you heard the song "Jesus Loves Me"? Probably so. It's a simple song that should remind you of this important fact: Jesus loves you very much.

When you invite Jesus into your heart, He'll love and protect you forever. If you have problems, He'll help you solve them. Even when you make mistakes or do something wrong, He still loves you. If you feel sorry or sad, He can help you feel better.

Jesus loves you. Simple, but so true. And that is awesome!

THOUGHT OF THE DAY

God made you special, and He loves you very much!

PRAY TODAY

Dear God, loving You is the best decision I could ever make. Thank You for filling my heart with strength, hope, and love. Amen.

TELL GOD THE TRUTH

If you hide your sins, you will not succeed. If you confess and reject them, you will receive mercy.

Proverbs 28:13 NCV

Some of the Bible's biggest heroes, like Peter and King David, also made big mistakes and disobeyed God. But God still used them! Does that surprise you?

It's actually very good news! Everyone makes mistakes, but God can use each one of us. All we need to do is be honest with God, tell Him what we did wrong, and ask Him to help us make things right. When your first goal is to love God and do what He wants, He can help you turn your mistake into a chance to praise Him!

THOUGHT OF THE DAY

God can use your mistakes for good!

PRAY TODAY

Dear God, thank You for forgiving me no matter what. I'm so glad I'll always be Your child! Amen.

SHOWING GOD'S LOVE

Little children, let us stop just saying we love people; let us really love them, and show it by our actions.

1 John 3:18 TLB

God loves us very much. One way He shows His love is by providing us with the things we need. He gives us wonderful gifts like friends and family, and food to eat.

God wants us to love others just like He loves us. It's important to tell people that we love them, but God wants us to show our love, too.

Your mom and dad show they love you by taking care of you and giving you a safe and loving home. Your friends show they love you by playing with you and sharing. Can you think of ways you can show your love to others? It will make God very happy!

THOUGHT OF THE DAY

If your actions are full of God's love, people will get the message!

PRAY TODAY

Dear God, thank You for Your love for me. Please help me show others how much You love them. Amen.

WORSHIP THE KING

Oh come, let us worship and bow down; let us kneel before the Lord, our Maker!

Psalm 95:6 ESV

Maybe you have seen pictures of kings or queens in a book. People around them treat them in a special way, bowing or kneeling before them.

The Bible says that God is the King of kings, meaning He is the most important King of all! He created the whole universe! You can show love and respect to God by talking to Him. You may even kneel beside your bed to pray at night, if you would like. He loves to hear you pray!

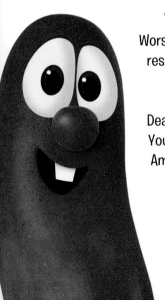

THOUGHT OF THE DAY

Worship means loving God and showing Him respect!

PRAY TODAY

Dear God, You are SO great! I will worship You and tell You how much I love You. Amen.

WHAT WOULD JESUS DO?

Follow God's example, therefore, as dearly loved children.

Ephesians 5:1 NIV

It seems like everyone wants to tell you how to act! Your favorite TV show might tell you one thing, while your friends tell you another. And it's tempting to follow along when it seems like everyone around you is making a certain choice! How can you know what's right?

When you read your Bible, pay attention to how Jesus acts. How does He treat people? What does He say when people are mean to Him? Anytime you wonder what to do, think about what Jesus would do in your situation. His way is always the best way!

THOUGHT OF THE DAY

What are some things Jesus did that seem unusual?

PRAY TODAY

Dear God, help me act like Jesus! I want to choose the right thing, even if it's hard. Amen.

A LIGHT IN THE DARKNESS

Jesus spoke to them again, saying, "I am the light of the world. He who follows Me shall not walk in darkness, but have the light of life."

John 8:12 NKJV

Have you ever lost something under the couch? It's so dark under there that it's hard to find anything! But if you shine a flashlight in the dark space, the darkness disappears and you can see everything clearly. All because of one light!

Jesus is like that flashlight. Sin makes the world dark, and we don't always know what to do. But when we follow Jesus, He makes our path bright so we can see where we're going and make good choices. So when you feel lost in the dark, just ask Jesus to shine His light!

THOUGHT OF THE DAY

Try shining a small flashlight into a dark space. How is this like Jesus' light?

PRAY TODAY

Dear God, I know Jesus came to light up the world! Help me follow Him closely so I'll always stay in His light. Amen.

PERFECT HARMONY

And above all these put on love, which binds everything together in perfect harmony.

Colossians 3:14 ESV

Sometimes people create a beautiful sound when they play music together. They do this by playing different notes that all work together at the same time. This is called harmony.

Families can have harmony too. Each person in the family is different. And when different members of your family love one another and work together, they create harmony. They can accomplish more together than each person could on his or her own. God loves it when a family works in perfect harmony.

What is special about each person in your family? Thank God for each person and the wonderful harmony that you create together.

THOUGHT OF THE DAY
Today, find a way to show someone in your family how much you love and appreciate him or her.

PRAY TODAY
Dear God, thank You for my family. Help me remember to always show love, especially when we have trouble getting along. Amen.

WHEN CHANGE IS HARD

There is a time for everything, and a season for every activity under the heavens.

Ecclesiastes 3:1 NIV

Things are always changing around us, and sometimes that can be hard. But we never have to worry because God is always ready to help us through the changes.

Maybe your family has to move to a new town. Or you are beginning a new grade at a new school. Or maybe you are starting a new activity and don't know anyone. You might feel a little excited, nervous, and uncertain—all at the same time!

Just remember that God knows where you are and how you are feeling. He is always with you, and you can trust in the Lord.

THOUGHT OF THE DAY
God is always there for you!

PRAY TODAY
Dear God, when things are changing, please help me to always look for You. Amen.

A POWERFUL SECRET

"But I say to you who listen: Love your enemies, do what is good to those who hate you, bless those who curse you, pray for those who mistreat you."

Luke 6:27-28 HCSB

Did you know that God forgives you, no matter what mistakes you make? Forgiveness is very important to God, and He wants us to forgive others just like He forgives us.

Forgiveness not only helps the person you forgive, it also helps you. When you forgive, you let go of the feelings of hurt and anger that can make you unhappy and sad. By letting go of those feelings, you can be happy and joyful.

So let go and forgive quickly. It's the best thing for everyone.

THOUGHT OF THE DAY

Forgiving someone can really make you feel better inside.

PRAY TODAY

Dear God, when others do things to hurt me, please help me forgive quickly. Amen.

GETTING TO KNOW HIM

Jesus said to him, "I am the way, and the truth, and the life. No one comes to the Father except through me."

John 14:6 ESV

There's really no way around it: if you want to know God, you need to know His Son. And that's good because getting to know Jesus is a wonderful thing! Jesus has an amazing love for you. Not only did He die for you, but because He came to earth to live just like us, He understands every problem and temptation you face.

Jesus desperately wants to introduce you to His Father and show you the life He has planned for you. So welcome Him into your heart today. You will be so glad you did!

THOUGHT OF THE DAY

What is your favorite story from the Bible about Jesus?

PRAY TODAY

Dear God, thank You for Jesus. He is my friend, and I want to know Him better every day. Amen.

MAGNIFY GOD!

"My soul magnifies the Lord, and my spirit has rejoiced in God my savior."

Luke 1:46b-47 NKJV

Have you ever used a magnifying glass? It's a special piece of glass that makes things look bigger. Even though the glass doesn't actually change the size of what you're looking at, it helps you see and understand it much better.

Your praise acts like a magnifying glass with God! Praising God doesn't change God's amazing size and power, but it helps you see Him more clearly. You'll feel His love more strongly and begin to see all the ways He has blessed you. So praise God today! Who knows what you'll discover?

THOUGHT OF THE DAY
Praising God can magnify Him for others, too!

PRAY TODAY
Dear God, I love You! I want to magnify You with praise every day! Amen.

PRAY FOR EVERYBODY

Love your enemies. Pray for those who hurt you.

Matthew 5:44 NCV

It's usually pretty easy to pray for your friends and family because those are the people you love most. But when it comes to praying for people who have hurt you, well that's a different thing entirely!

The Bible tells us that God wants us to pray for the folks we don't like, too. Why? God wants you to do it because He knows it's really the best thing for you. And your prayers might just make a big difference for them, too!

THOUGHT OF THE DAY

What's the secret to forgiving others? Remember all the things God has forgiven you for.

PRAY TODAY

Dear God, I know forgiving others is important to You. So please give me a forgiving heart, Lord. Amen.

KEEP BELIEVING

Immediately the father of the child cried out and said with tears, "Lord, I believe; help my unbelief!"

Mark 9:24 NKJV

Are you the type of kid who has lots and lots of questions? Do most of them start with "Why"? If so, you'll be glad to know that you can ask God anything and everything!

God has all kinds of answers for you, and you can find many of them in the Bible. Sometimes, though, the answers don't come right away, and things can be hard to understand.

But in those moments, trust in God and keep believing. God won't let you down.

THOUGHT OF THE DAY

Trust in God, no matter what.

PRAY TODAY

Dear God, I know that I can't understand everything that happens. But I trust You. Help me stay strong. Amen.

JUST KEEP TRYING

The Lord says, "Forget what happened before, and do not think about the past. Look at the new thing I am going to do. It is already happening. Don't you see it?"

Isaiah 43:18-19 NCV

It can be frustrating to make mistakes. But don't worry! Jesus is the only person who ever lived a perfect life, and His sacrifice means that we can be forgiven for every mistake we make.

Ask for forgiveness and ask God to help you learn what you need to learn. Don't ever give up! When you ask God to help you, He will be there with you! God's faithfulness and love are forever.

THOUGHT OF THE DAY

Trust in God to help you keep on learning from Him and to keep making new things happen in your heart.

PRAY TODAY

Dear God, help me to trust Your love and Your work in me. Amen.

HOW WILL THEY KNOW?

"This is how everyone will recognize that you are my disciples—when they see the love you have for each other."

John 13:35 MSG

How do people know that you love God? Well, you can tell them, of course. And talking about your faith in God is a very good thing to do. But Jesus said people would be able to tell that you follow Him by doing one simple thing: loving others.

Loving people isn't always easy. But choosing to love someone even when it's hard is exactly the moment when God shines the brightest in you.

Today, look for ways to show God's love to the people you meet. They'll know something is different about you!

THOUGHT OF THE DAY

Write down three things you can do for someone you know who can be hard to love!

PRAY TODAY

Dear God, I want people to be able to tell that I know You. Help me show love to others all the time. Amen.

YOUR VERY BEST FRIEND!

Then Jesus said, "I am the bread that gives life. Whoever comes to me will never be hungry, and whoever believes in me will never be thirsty."

John 6:35 NCV

Do you have a best friend? Someone you love to hang out with and who likes the same stuff you do? Maybe you have a couple of great friends!

When you invite Jesus into your heart, you get a new best friend—forever. If you make mistakes, He'll still be your friend. If you behave badly, He'll still love you. If you feel sorry or sad, He can help you feel better.

Jesus is everything you will ever want or need. Hang out with Him today!

THOUGHT OF THE DAY

What are three things a best friend should always do?

PRAY TODAY

Dear God, I am so glad that Jesus loves me and is my very best friend. Amen.

KEEP IT UP!

So don't get tired of doing what is good. Don't get discouraged and give up, for we will reap a harvest of blessing at the appropriate time.

Galatians 6:9 NLT

The Bible teaches us to treat other people with respect, kindness, courtesy, and love. You might wonder sometimes if anybody notices when you do these things or if it really makes a difference. Well, it does!

The Bible says we shouldn't get tired of doing the right thing. If we keep treating others the way we are supposed to, God will reward us when the time is right. God always sees your efforts, and He is pleased and proud of you. So don't quit . . . keep it up!

THOUGHT OF THE DAY

Doing the right thing always makes you feel great.

PRAY TODAY

Dear God, please help me to keep doing what You want me to do. I won't give up. Amen.

A SONG FOR GOD

Sing to the LORD a new song; sing to the LORD, all the earth. Sing to the LORD and praise his name; every day tell how he saves us.

Psalm 96:1-2 NCV

Praising God means celebrating how great He is. It is one of the most important things you can do. And it's also fun!

God loves to hear you praise Him with music. You can sing a song to tell God how much you love Him. You can use the wonderful body He gave you to dance for Him. You can beat a drum or shake a tambourine, ring a bell or play a tune on a harmonica! However you choose to praise God is just right. God wants to hear your special song!

THOUGHT OF THE DAY

How can you praise God with music today?

PRAY TODAY

Dear God, You are so great! Help me find new ways to praise You every day. Amen.

A GREAT DAY TO BE HAPPY

This is the day the LORD has made; let us rejoice and be glad in it.

Psalm 118:24 HCSB

Every new day, including this one, is a wonderful treasure. Today is a priceless gift from God, and He wants you to think of it that way.

Whether you realize it or not, you have more things to be thankful for than you can count. But it never hurts to try counting them anyway.

God has given you so much, so remember to thank Him today. Make an effort to find one or two things to be happy about today—no matter how small they are!

THOUGHT OF THE DAY

Each day is like a new, unopened present. You never know what you will find inside!

PRAY TODAY

Dear God, thank You for Your gift of today. It's so good to be happy! Amen.

GO TELL IT

All who worship God, come here and listen; I will tell you everything God has done for me.

Psalm 66:16 CEV

Everyone loves a good story. It's fun to listen to and fun to tell. God made you special, and He has a special story that you can share with others. That story is simply telling others how much you love God and about His love for you.

Be glad that you can share your story with others. Maybe your story can help someone else learn about God.

That would be extra special!

THOUGHT OF THE DAY

Go tell others the happy news of God and His love!

PRAY TODAY

Dear God, thank You for loving me. Help me to share my story with others so they can love You too. Amen.

FINDING GOD

But from there, you will search for the L<small>ORD</small> your God, and you will find Him when you seek Him with all your heart and all your soul.

Deuteronomy 4:29 H<small>CSB</small>

God wants us to know Him and have a relationship where we trust and follow Him.

He created beautiful things in nature that we can see every day. He shows us His love through our family and friends. He gives us the Bible, which shows us how He wants us to live.

You can trust that He is there and that He cares for you.

THOUGHT OF THE DAY

God helps us to want to know and trust Him.

PRAY TODAY

Dear God, I know that You are there. Thank You for caring for me. Amen.

BE STRONG

Wait for the LORD; be strong, and let your heart take courage; wait for the LORD!

Psalm 27:14 ESV

Do you know what the heroes of the Bible had in common? When really bad stuff started to happen, they didn't give up. They chose to be brave and strong. And they put their trust in God and waited for His help.

When Noah faced the flood, he followed God's plan to build a boat and trusted that God would save his family. And when David fought Goliath, he knew that he would win because God was on his side.

If you have a problem you think is too big to solve, turn to God for help. He will always be there for you.

THOUGHT OF THE DAY

God's help is always a prayer away!

PRAY TODAY

Dear God, I don't always feel very brave or courageous, but I can wait for You. Thank You for always coming to my rescue. Amen.

DO THE RIGHT THING

"So don't worry, because I am with you. . . . I will make you strong and will help you."

Isaiah 41:10 NCV

Doing what God says isn't always easy. But you never have to do it alone! God can help.

Sometimes He asks you to do things, like talk to a new kid at school, tell the truth, or help someone. You may have to stand up to your friends when you disagree with what they are choosing. You make God happy when you choose to do what's right, even when it's hard. Ask for His help, and He will give you courage to choose the right thing every time.

THOUGHT OF THE DAY

Can you think of a time when it was hard to do the right thing?

PRAY TODAY

Dear God, please give me courage to do what's right. Sometimes it's hard, but I want to make You happy. Amen.

IT'S GOOD TO HAVE GOOD FRIENDS

My dear, dear friends, if God loved us like this, we certainly ought to love each other.

1 John 4:11 MSG

One of the best gifts God will ever give you is a good, kind friend. Do you have some good and kind friends in your life? How do they help you? What do you do to help them?

Be thankful today for the good friends you have. And show them how much you appreciate them by being a good friend to them, too.

THOUGHT OF THE DAY

Never forget to thank God for your friends!

PRAY TODAY

Dear God, thank You for my friends, and help me to be the best friend I can be. Amen.

GOD WILL LEAD THE WAY

During the day the LORD went ahead of his people in a thick cloud, and during the night he went ahead of them in a flaming fire.

Exodus 13:21 CEV

After Moses led the people of Israel out of Egypt, God performed many miracles to take care of them.

God parted the Red Sea so that they could cross safely. He fed them with manna from heaven. He sent a tall cloud, which changed into a ball of fire at night, to guide the people and to show them that He was always with them.

God is always there for you, too. You may not see a ball of fire in the sky, but He will lead you where you need to go.

THOUGHT OF THE DAY

The Bible says that God's Word is a light for your path.

PRAY TODAY

Dear God, thank You for leading me and guiding me with Your Word. Amen.

THE FRUIT OF LIGHT

Walk as children of light (for the fruit of light is found in all that is good and right and true).

Ephesians 5:8-9 ESV

Do you like fruit? Most fruit tastes good. And it's good for you too. The Bible tells us about a different kind of fruit—the fruit of the Spirit. This is the fruit that we grow when we are filled with God's love.

What are the fruits of the Spirit? Love, joy, peace, patience, kindness, goodness, faithfulness, gentleness, and self-control.

These fruits are all good traits, and God wants to see them in you too! Live every day as a child of God, and you will grow good fruit that others will be able to see!

THOUGHT OF THE DAY

Nobody produces fruit overnight. It takes time, so don't give up!

PRAY TODAY

Dear God, I want to know and love You better so all of the fruit of the Spirit is in me. Amen.

GOD'S GIFTS

Whatever is good and perfect is a gift coming down to us from God our Father, who created all the lights in the heavens. He never changes or casts a shifting shadow.

James 1:17 NLT

Have you said "thank You" to God today? God has given us many gifts and blessings in our lives, and for that we are thankful!

God has given you a family and friends. He gives you food to eat and a warm, loving home. Your church and neighborhood and fun activities are all gifts from God. Even school is a blessing!

Take time today to think about the things that mean the most to you, and remember to thank God for all of His good and perfect gifts to you.

THOUGHT OF THE DAY

God is good all the time.

PRAY TODAY

Dear God, thank You for giving me so many wonderful gifts. Help me remember to thank You every day. Amen.

FOLLOW GOD'S DIRECTIONS

Now, Israel, listen to the laws and commands I will teach you. Obey them so that you will live.

Deuteronomy 4:1 NCV

D o you know the story of Jonah? God asked him to go to a town called Ninevah and tell everyone there to follow God. But Jonah didn't want to go, so he tried to run away. He even jumped into the sea, but God sent a big fish to bring him to dry land! Finally, Jonah decided to obey God. He went to Ninevah, said what God told him to say, and everyone decided to follow God. Jonah saved a whole town that day!

When it's hard to obey God, remember Jonah's story. God's ways are always best!

THOUGHT OF THE DAY

It's always best to obey God the first time He asks!

PRAY TODAY

Dear God, help me to obey Your directions. I trust that You will be with me! Amen.

A LIGHT OF KINDNESS

Let everyone see that you are gentle and kind. The Lord is coming soon.

Philippians 4:5 NCV

The Bible tells us that Jesus is coming back soon! Until He comes, God wants us to be gentle and kind to everyone.

Showing kindness to others is an important job! People need to know how much God loves them and that He can help them when they are in trouble. And they learn about God's love by watching you. So keep it up—your light is shining!

THOUGHT OF THE DAY

Think of someone you can show kindness to today.

PRAY TODAY

Dear God, help me shine Your light in the darkness and show people how much You love them. Amen.

A SAFE PLACE

You are my hiding place and my shield; I hope in your word.

Psalm 119:114 NCV

God wants to give you courage and strength to do great things! But did you know He can also be a hiding place?

When you feel afraid or overwhelmed, you can go to God in prayer and rest with Him. Sometimes it helps to imagine climbing onto His lap or snuggling next to Him in a big comfy chair. You can also think about other ways the Bible describes God—as a shelter in a rainstorm, or a sturdy place to stand when everything else is shaky. God is always with you. He is your special, safe hiding place.

THOUGHT OF THE DAY

It's impossible to hide from God, but you can always hide in God.

PRAY TODAY

Dear God, thank You for welcoming me into Your arms. Help me find rest in You. Amen.

RESPECT EVERYONE

Show respect for all people. Love the brothers and sisters of God's family.

1 Peter 2:17 ICB

It's important to respect people who are in charge, like your parents and your teachers. But God wants us to treat *everyone* with respect. Respecting people means to treat them like they matter. And people matter to God.

Jesus showed respect to everyone He met, rich or poor. He respected His disciples by answering their questions and spending time with them. He even respected people nobody else liked because He knew that God loves everyone. When you show respect to others, you're acting like Jesus!

THOUGHT OF THE DAY

How can you show respect to the people you'll meet today?

PRAY TODAY

Dear God, You love everyone! Please help me show respect to everyone around me. Amen.

LAUGH OUT LOUD

"He will yet fill your mouth with laughter and your lips with shouts of joy."

Job 8:21 NIV

Sometimes we might think that God is only super serious. God is also full of joy, and He loves it when you laugh and play!

God tells us throughout the Bible to rejoice. Rejoicing is not sad and serious—it is joyful and happy. So whether you feel excited about something God has done for you or just want to do something fun today, make time to laugh out loud. Your heart will be glad you did!

THOUGHT OF THE DAY

Laughter is a wonderful gift from God.

PRAY TODAY

Dear God, thank You for giving me the gift of laughter. I will laugh with You today. Amen.

HONOR GOD

"You shall have no other gods before me."

Exodus 20:3 ESV

God gave the Ten Commandments to Moses. These were the laws that God wanted His people to follow so they could be safe and happy.

The first three commandments talk about the most important thing of all: having a relationship with God.

What are those first three commandments? First, love God more than anything else. Second, make God the most important thing in your life. And third, always say God's name with love and respect. Those are wonderful rules to live by!

THOUGHT OF THE DAY

Make God the most important part of your life!

PRAY TODAY

Dear God, please help me to put You first. I want to love You, honor You, and always show You respect. Amen.

THINK BEFORE YOU SPEAK

A kind answer soothes angry feelings, but harsh words stir them up.

Proverbs 15:1 CEV

Words are very powerful! They can encourage or they can hurt feelings. So you have to be careful when you use them.

When you're angry, it's especially easy to say things you might feel bad about later. So take a deep breath and think carefully before you say anything. Try replacing any angry words with kind words instead. That will keep you from hurting anyone's feelings, and it could also help solve the problem. Wise King Solomon tells us that angry words only make an argument worse. So be part of the solution instead!

THOUGHT OF THE DAY

Practice kind responses so you can be ready for any conversation.

PRAY TODAY

Dear God, it's hard to think when I get angry. Help me pause and think before I speak. Amen.

FRIEND OF GOD

"You are my friends, if you obey me. Servants don't know what their master is doing, and so I don't speak to you as my servants. I speak to you as my friends, and I have told you everything that my Father has told me."

John 15:14-15 CEV

Did you know that Jesus said you are His friend? That's amazing to think about, isn't it? And it's true! The Bible tells us that Jesus said we are His friends if we love Him and obey Him. That's a really big deal. That means when you are in trouble, God has your back. He will never leave you or forsake you. No matter what happens, God will be there for you. Can you imagine anything better than being a friend of God?

THOUGHT OF THE DAY

How does knowing that God is your friend make you feel about yourself?

PRAY TODAY

Dear God, I am so glad to be Your friend. Thank You for making me feel special and loved. Amen.

LIVING THE GOOD LIFE

I have chosen the way of faithfulness; I set your rules before me.

Psalm 119:30 ESV

God has rules for living, and He really wants you to obey them. He wants you to be fair, honest, and kind. He wants you to behave well, and He wants you to respect your parents.

Why does God want you to do all these things? Well, it's because He wants you to live a life that is happy and blessed, and He wants you to honor Him with how you live and the choices you make. That way people will see God's love when they see you!

THOUGHT OF THE DAY

God wants you to do the right things because it's the best thing for you!

PRAY TODAY

Dear God, please help me pay attention to the rules that You want me to follow so my life can be the best it can be. Amen.

THINGS TO TALK ABOUT

There is a time for everything. . . . a time to be silent and a time to speak.

Ecclesiastes 3:1, 7 NIV

Do you have lots and lots of things to talk about? Sometimes it can be really hard to keep exciting, happy, or curious thoughts to yourself! But what do you do if you are in a place where you need to sit still and quiet, like at school or church?

The Bible talks about being kind and respectful of others. That means that sometimes you might need to wait a little bit to ask questions or talk about your news.

What you have to say matters, so if you need to talk, ask your parents or teachers when they will be able to listen. You'll be glad you did!

THOUGHT OF THE DAY

Sometimes the best thing you can do for a friend is be quiet and listen.

PRAY TODAY

Dear God, help me to know when it's time for me to speak and when it's time to be quiet. Amen.

PRACTICE MAKES PATIENCE

Be gentle to everyone, able to teach, and patient.

2 Timothy 2:24 HCSB

God talks about patience a lot in the Bible. It must be very important! But it's not always easy.

That's because patience takes lots of practice. Sometimes patience means waiting for someone to finish playing with a toy that you want. Sometimes it means not complaining while your mom or dad finishes shopping at the grocery store. Sometimes it means listening to someone else's story before you get to tell yours. Next time you feel impatient, take a deep breath and ask God to help you wait. That's practicing patience. And the more you practice, the better you'll be!

THOUGHT OF THE DAY

Think of a time you needed to be patient. What did you do?

PRAY TODAY

Dear God, I know You want me to be patient, but sometimes it's so hard. Please help me practice so I can get better! Amen.

LEARN FROM YOUR MISTAKES

No one in this world always does right.

Ecclesiastes 7:20 CEV

Do you make mistakes? Of course you do. Everybody does. When you make a mistake, the important thing is to try your best to learn from it so that you won't make the very same mistake again. And if you have hurt someone or disappointed God or someone close to you, you should ask for forgiveness.

Remember: mistakes are a part of life. Some mistakes are bigger than others, but no one can say they always do the right thing. So don't worry! Just keep trying to do better next time.

THOUGHT OF THE DAY

If you make a mistake, don't try to deny it! Just admit it and move on.

PRAY TODAY

Dear God, help me learn from my mistakes so that I can be a better person. Amen.

A KIND WORD

How wonderful it is to be able to say the right thing at the right time!

Proverbs 15:23 TLB

Saying kind words is one of the best ways to show God's love. And it's so easy! All you have to do is pay attention.

As you go through your day, look for people who need to hear something kind. Is someone left out on the playground? Does a friend feel sad today? Would your mom or dad like to hear you say that you appreciate the dinner they made? If you keep asking, God will show you people who need your kindness. And when you obey His guidance, you will make lots of people happy!

THOUGHT OF THE DAY

A kind word is always welcome.

PRAY TODAY

Dear God, please help me share kind words today. I want to make people happy! Amen.

GOD GUIDES YOUR STEPS

A man's heart plans his way, but the Lord determines his steps.

Proverbs 16:9 HCSB

What do you want to be when you grow up? A pilot or a musician? A doctor or a scientist? Maybe you want to work with computers or become a teacher.

Whatever it is that you hope to do, you should know one thing: God has great plans for you! You should do your very best at school, and if you have a dream, give it everything you have. And don't forget to pray and ask God to guide you. Follow His lead, and you will become the person He made you to be.

THOUGHT OF THE DAY

God holds your future in His hands.

PRAY TODAY

Dear God, I am excited about my future. Please guide my steps and lead me into Your perfect plan. Amen.

THE WAY, THE TRUTH, AND THE LIFE

Jesus answered, "I am the way and the truth and the life. No one comes to the Father except through me."

John 14:6 NIV

The Bible tells us that there is only one way to meet God: through His Son, Jesus.

Jesus is the Way, the Truth, and the Life. Because Jesus died for you, your sins are forgiven! So He makes the way for you to go to God yourself, without fear or worry. Through Jesus, you can know and love God, the Father, the way He has always wanted you to.

Open your heart to Jesus today!

THOUGHT OF THE DAY

If Jesus says it's the truth, then it's the truth!

PRAY TODAY

Dear God, thank You for sending Jesus. I want to follow Him and know You more every day. Amen.

KEEP GOING!

Noah was another who trusted God. When he heard God's warning about the future, Noah believed him even though there was then no sign of a flood, and wasting no time, he built the ark and saved his family.

Hebrews 11:7 TLB

D o you remember the story of Noah? God told him to build a boat big enough to hold his family and every kind of animal because a flood was coming that would destroy everything on the earth.

People thought Noah was crazy. They didn't believe what he said could happen. They made fun of Noah and ignored God's warning.

But what did Noah do? He believed God and built a boat. A huge boat. It took him a long time, but he kept working. And when the flood came, he was ready.

THOUGHT OF THE DAY

Do you think Noah wanted to give up? What made him keep going?

PRAY TODAY

Dear God, I want to believe You like Noah did. Please help me to keep going, even when things seem impossible. Amen.

GOD CAN USE YOU

Every good gift and every perfect gift is from above, coming down from the Father of lights.

James 1:17 NKJV

Every good gift in your life is from God! That means your family, your friends, your home, your stuff, your talents, your favorite things to do, and even your favorite birthday present are all blessings sent to you from your Heavenly Father.

God wants you to share your blessings with others. For example, you can share your toys, take time to help someone learn to tie his or her shoes, or help clean up a mess. Sometimes when you do something nice or share something God has given you, it feels so good that the act of sharing can be a gift of its own!

THOUGHT OF THE DAY
Helping other people can feel so good!

PRAY TODAY
Dear God, thank You for all of the good gifts You have given me. I want You to use me to help others too. Amen.

ALWAYS WITH YOU

"I will be with you always, even until the end of the world."

Matthew 28:20 CEV

The Bible tells us that no matter where we are, God is with us. Always!

That's pretty amazing to think about. Part of growing up means you'll be going to new places and trying new things. But you never go anywhere alone because God is with you, even though you can't see Him.

God's Word is there to remind us that if we are afraid or worried, we can know that God is with us and He will take care of us.

THOUGHT OF THE DAY

Always remember that God is with you wherever you go.

PRAY TODAY

Dear God, I am so glad that You never leave me and are always with me. Amen.

HEAVENLY PEACE

"I leave you peace. My peace I give you. I do not give it to you as the world does. So don't let your hearts be troubled."

John 14:27 ICB

The Bible tells us that Jesus offers us peace, not like what the world gives, but a peace that is perfect. We can either accept His peace or ignore it.

When we accept the peace of Jesus Christ into our hearts, our lives are changed forever. Peace is God's gift to you; it is yours for the asking.

Ask Jesus for His peace. He is happy to give it to you!

THOUGHT OF THE DAY

You can handle anything if God's peace is in your heart!

PRAY TODAY

Dear God, I want to receive the special peace that You have to give me and then share it with others. Amen.

NO MATTER WHAT

Your name will be Abraham, for I have made you a father of many nations.

Genesis 17:5 HCSB

Abraham was a man who loved God and believed what He said—no matter what. When God promised to make Abraham the "father of many nations," Abraham was already very old. Too old, many thought, for him to ever be the father to one child—let alone enough to fill many nations!

But Abraham believed God. He knew that when God makes a promise, He always keeps it.

It took a little while, but just like God promised, Abraham had a son. And now, thousands of years later, his descendants are all around the world!

THOUGHT OF THE DAY

If God makes a promise, you can count on it!

PRAY TODAY

Dear God, I want to have faith like Abraham. Help me trust You no matter what. Amen.

LAUGH TOGETHER

How we laughed and sang for joy. And the other nations said, "What amazing things the Lord has done for them."

Psalm 126:2 TLB

What makes you laugh? Do you like to tell jokes or sing silly songs? What about making funny faces? Laughing is so much fun, and it can make any day bright!

God wants us to be so happy that we laugh a lot! Laughing is a gift we can all enjoy. Laughing at someone instead of with them is not a good kind of laughter. Laughter is best when no one is hurt by it and it makes our hearts happy.

THOUGHT OF THE DAY

Larry loves to laugh and be silly! What silly things make you laugh?

PRAY TODAY

Dear God, I love to laugh! Help me share laughter with my friends and family today. Amen.

HE ANSWERS

*For I know the thoughts that I think toward you, says the L*ORD*, thoughts of peace and not of evil, to give you a future and a hope. Then you will call upon Me and go and pray to Me, and I will listen to you.*

Jeremiah 29:11-12 NKJV

D o you ever wonder if God really answers your prayers? The answer is yes! But the answer may come in a different way than you expect.

Sometimes, God may not answer your prayers as fast as you would like. Or the answer may not be what you think He will say. Many times God says yes, but sometimes He says no.

Fortunately, God has a plan, and He's got everything under control. So keep praying, and when the time is right, He'll answer!

THOUGHT OF THE DAY

Don't worry about whether your words are the right words. Just talk to God from your heart.

PRAY TODAY

Dear God, thank You for always listening to my prayers. I know You will give me the answer I need. Amen.

IN LINE WITH JESUS

"Follow Me," Jesus told them, "and I will make you fish for people!" Immediately they left their nets and followed Him.

Mark 1:17-18 HCSB

When you're walking in a line, the first person leads everyone else where they should go. So, it's pretty important for that person to know the right way!

Jesus told people to follow Him because He knew the right way for them to go. He wanted His followers to care for others, showing people the way to God. He wanted them to make loving choices. As they followed Jesus, they were blessed and they brought blessings to others too. It's a good idea to walk closely with Jesus every day. He knows the way to your very best life!

THOUGHT OF THE DAY

What's one thing you can do today that Jesus would do?

PRAY TODAY

Dear God, I want to follow Jesus every day of my life. Help me share His love with everyone I know. Amen.

GOOD RULES

Practice God's law—get a reputation for wisdom.

Proverbs 28:7 MSG

God made you to be a special part of His world. And He gives us all good rules to follow so we can live the life He wants us to have.

Following God's rules takes practice. Just like you have to play a game several times before you can do it well, you can work on God's rules every day. Don't worry if you make a mistake! Just decide what you want to do differently, and try that next time. Pretty soon, you'll be in the good habit of following good rules!

THOUGHT OF THE DAY

Before you speak or act, ask yourself, "Will this make God happy?"

PRAY TODAY

Dear God, please help me stop and think before I make decisions. I want to be good at following Your rules! Amen.

GIVE GOD YOUR WORRIES

Give all your worries and cares to God, for he cares about what happens to you.

1 Peter 5:6 NLT

The Bible says we should give all of our cares to God. He is more than able to handle any problem, and He loves you so much that He is glad to do it.

What things are going on with you today? Whatever it is, God knows everything that is happening to you, and He cares about every little detail. So why not let God take care of it?

THOUGHT OF THE DAY

Close your eyes, and imagine handing God a box full of everything you care about.

PRAY TODAY

Dear God, I know You can handle anything that happens and that You care for me. Amen.

GOD BEFORE STUFF

Seek first God's kingdom and what God wants. Then all your other needs will be met as well.

Matthew 6:33 NCV

It's normal to want stuff we don't have. Maybe a friend has a new toy you want to play with, or a book you'd like to read. But trouble comes if you think about stuff more than you think about God!

Stuff is nice for a little while, but God is with you forever. He is more important than anything you could buy, and He has promised to take care of you! So don't worry about what you don't have. Spend time thanking God for what He has given you and doing things that make Him happy. You'll realize that stuff doesn't matter as much!

THOUGHT OF THE DAY

When you want something new, first thank God for what you already have!

PRAY TODAY

Dear God, thank You for everything You've given me! Help me focus on You instead of things. Amen.

TIME TO LISTEN

Be still before the Lord and wait patiently for him.

Psalm 37:7 NIV

Have you ever not heard something someone just said? Maybe you were playing with your dog, or running after a ball, or looking the other way—you weren't listening, so you couldn't hear what they said.

Sometimes it's like that with God. We can't hear what He might be saying to us. If you spend a little time being quiet and waiting for God to speak, you'll be able to hear Him much better.

Being quiet is hard for many of us, and being patient can be even harder! But don't give up. God wants to talk with you. If you make time for Him, He'll "show up."

THOUGHT OF THE DAY

Decide on a time to pray quietly for five minutes every day. God will love spending time with you!

PRAY TODAY

Dear God, help me to be still and listen to You. I want to spend time with You every day! Amen.

KEEP PRAYING

"Continue to ask, and God will give to you. Continue to search, and you will find. Continue to knock, and the door will open for you."

Matthew 7:7 ICB

God loves to hear from you. He wants you to share your thoughts with Him and ask for His help. You can ask God for anything! Maybe you'd like to make a new friend, or you're trying to find ways to help out in your neighborhood. Maybe you need to say you're sorry to someone, but it's hard. Maybe you're working on learning something new. God can help you! Sometimes God answers prayers quickly, but other times His answers take longer. Don't give up! Keep on praying. God promises that He will always answer.

THOUGHT OF THE DAY

What is something you need God's help with today?

PRAY TODAY

Dear God, thank You for listening to all my prayers. Please help me remember to keep on praying! Amen.

HOW GOD SEES YOU

I praise you because you made me in an amazing and wonderful way. What you have done is wonderful. I know this very well.

Psalm 139:14 ICB

What does God see when He looks at you? A kind-hearted, amazing, talented kid! He knows better than anyone else who you really are and what is special about you.

God knows you the best. He made you in His image and gave you gifts that are all your own. And He thinks you are wonderful!

Always remember: God made you special, and He loves you very much!

THOUGHT OF THE DAY

God made you special!

PRAY TODAY

Dear God, thank You for making me who I am. Help me to see myself the way You see me. Amen.

MORE THAN YOU CAN COUNT!

Then Peter came to him and asked, "Lord, how often should I forgive someone who sins against me? Seven times?" "No!" Jesus replied, "seventy times seven!"

Matthew 18:21-22 NLT

How often does God forgive us? More times than we can count! And that, by the way, is exactly how many times that God expects us to forgive other people—more times than we can count!

Forgiveness is one of the best ways to show God's love to other people!

THOUGHT OF THE DAY

Don't try to do the math . . . the numbers can get pretty big. Just keep on forgiving!

PRAY TODAY

Dear God, help me to keep on forgiving others, just as You have forgiven me. Amen.

GIVE FREELY

Freely you have received; freely give.

Matthew 10:8 NIV

God has given you many gifts, but He doesn't expect anything back. Isn't that wonderful? That's what it means to "give freely." And He wants us to give freely to each other as well.

Think of what you can give to others. Of course, it's nice to give gifts on birthdays and Christmas, but you don't have to wait! Ask your parents how to give away nice toys or clothes you don't use anymore. Make a card to tell a friend how much you like them. And you can always give a hug to someone who feels sad. Giving gifts isn't about getting something back. It's about sharing God's love!

THOUGHT OF THE DAY

What is something you can give away today?

PRAY TODAY

Dear God, thank You for all the gifts You have given to me. Help me give to others like You have given to me! Amen.

A LOVE HABIT

Dear friends, let us practice loving each other, for love comes from God and those who are loving and kind show that they are the children of God, and that they are getting to know him better.

1 John 4:7 TLB

Love takes practice. Why? Because real love—giving to others, putting others first, and not thinking about ourselves—may not come naturally to us most of the time.

Love comes naturally to God because He *is* love. But we have to practice loving people God's way, which becomes easier the more we spend time with God and get to know Him.

Can you think of any habit that could be better than loving others? Start practicing today, and love like God loves!

THOUGHT OF THE DAY

Look for something you can do for someone else today.

PRAY TODAY

Dear God, I want to love the way You love. Please help me to learn to love others better every day. Amen.

GOD IS WITH YOU

"Do not fear, for I am with you; do not be afraid, for I am your God. I will strengthen you; I will help you; I will hold on to you with My righteous right hand."

Isaiah 41:10 HCSB

Do you know that the Bible tells us exactly where God is? He's with you!

That might surprise you, because you can't see God like you can see your mom or dad. But it's true! God promises that He will be with you no matter where you go, and God always keeps His promises. So you never need to feel lonely or afraid. God is bigger and stronger than anything, and He's by your side today, tomorrow, and forever.

THOUGHT OF THE DAY

With God beside you, you can do anything!

PRAY TODAY

Dear God, please help me remember that You are always with me. Thank You for keeping Your promises! Amen.

CONFIDENCE AND TRUST

Let your steadfast love, O Lᴏʀᴅ, be upon us, even as we hope in you.

Psalm 33:22 ᴇsᴠ

The Bible says that God has great plans for you. You are going to have an amazing future and do incredible things! But there will be days when you wonder if things are going right. Everybody has hard days . . . and that is when we need hope!

To hope means to have confidence and trust, and there is no one we can have more confidence or trust in than God. When you start to feel discouraged, choose to trust God. Remember how much He loves you, and never give up.

THOUGHT OF THE DAY
What do you hope God will do for you in the future?

PRAY TODAY
Dear God, I will choose to trust You in everything. My hope is in You. Amen.

GOD'S TIMING

He has made everything beautiful in its time.

Ecclesiastes 3:11 NIV

Sometimes God answers prayers quickly, and sometimes His answers take longer. Sometimes His answers look different from what you expect. But you can always be sure that God is working to give you the very best life.

It can be really hard to wait for something you want, but don't worry! You can spend that time looking for ways that God is already working. He is always doing great things! God has big, wonderful plans for you, and He knows exactly when everything should happen. So keep praying, then watch God's plans unfold.

THOUGHT OF THE DAY

God is always right on time!

PRAY TODAY

Dear God, sometimes I want things to happen right away. Please remind me that Your timing is perfect. Amen.

WHAT A FRIEND!

"Just as the Father has loved Me, I have also loved you; abide in My love."

John 15:9 NASB

Do you know what friendship is about? Every true friendship should have kindness, thoughtfulness, love, and sharing. And there is no one who has given more of those things to you than Jesus.

That's right! Jesus is your friend. In fact, He's your very best friend of all.

Just like your other friends, Jesus wants to spend time with you. He wants to talk with you and listen to what you are excited about or the problems you are having. He cares about you more than anything. So don't forget to spend time with Him—there is no friend like Jesus!

THOUGHT OF THE DAY

Isn't it great that Jesus loves you so much?

PRAY TODAY

Dear God, I am glad that Jesus is my friend. Help me to remember to spend time with Him and be the best friend I can be. Amen.

THINK OF OTHERS FIRST

Don't be selfish. . . . Be humble, thinking of others as better than yourself.

Philippians 2:3 TLB

Jesus was the most important person who ever lived. But He didn't brag, and He wasn't selfish. Instead, He thought of others' feelings before His own. That's called being humble.

God wants us to be humble too. You can be humble by letting someone else go before you in line, or by being a good listener even when you want to say something. When you're humble, you show that God is most important. And it helps everyone around you feel good too!

THOUGHT OF THE DAY

To be humble, think about how others feel before you think about yourself.

PRAY TODAY

Dear God, it's not always easy to be humble. Please help me think of others first, just like Jesus did! Amen.

WHO IS YOUR NEIGHBOR?

If you really fulfill the royal law according to the Scripture, "You shall love your neighbor as yourself," you are doing well.

James 2:8 ESV

The Bible tells us we should love our neighbors as ourselves, but who is God talking about?

Neighbors can be people who live on your street or in your neighborhood, but they're not the only ones. Your neighbors are all those God brings across your path. They are the people you go to school with, the people in your church, the people in the checkout line at the store, and even people who live in other places!

Wherever you meet your neighbors, you can show love in all kinds of ways. So who is your neighbor today?

THOUGHT OF THE DAY

How can you love the "neighbors" you've never even met? You can pray for them!

PRAY TODAY

Dear God, help me remember that all those I meet are my neighbors, so I can love them as I love myself. Amen.

BE BRAVE!

"Don't worry about this Philistine," David told Saul. "I'll go fight him!"

1 Samuel 17:32 NLT

The next time you're reading your Bible, check out the story of David and Goliath. Goliath was a big, strong soldier who was saying bad things about God's people. Everyone was afraid to fight him, but David knew what Goliath was doing was wrong. So even though David wasn't a soldier, he used whatever God gave him to stand up for what was right.

God helped David be brave so he could face Goliath. He can make you brave, too! If you see something happening that seems wrong, ask God for the courage to fix it. God can help you do anything!

THOUGHT OF THE DAY
Trust God, and He will help you be brave!

PRAY TODAY
Dear God, please give me courage to do hard things. I can do anything by Your side. Amen.

CHOOSE YOUR WORDS

Be gracious in your speech. The goal is to bring out the best in others in a conversation, not put them down, not cut them out.

Colossians 4:6 MSG

Have you ever heard someone say, "Think before you speak"? That's because when you speak, you can really affect someone—you can choose to help, hurt, encourage, or ignore.

Use your words for good. When you speak, think about how you'd like people to talk to you. Offer praise for a job well done and encouragement in tough times. And when you talk about someone who is not there, be sure to follow the same rules. Speaking kindly is always the best choice. Don't be surprised if other people follow your example!

THOUGHT OF THE DAY

Once you speak, your words are out there and cannot be put back in your mouth. So choose words that make things better!

PRAY TODAY

Dear God, help me think before I speak. I want to choose words that make You and others happy! Amen.

CELEBRATE FRIENDS

Every time I think of you, I give thanks to my God.

Philippians 1:3 NLT

Isn't it great to have friends? A good friend can cheer you up when you feel sad or share a laugh when you're feeling silly. Sometimes a friend can teach you how to do something new! And no matter how many friends you have, you can always make more.

Good friends are a gift from God, so remember to thank Him for all the special friends in your life. And be sure to tell your friends how much you love them, too!

THOUGHT OF THE DAY

What are some things you like to do with your friends?

PRAY TODAY

Dear God, thank You for my friends. What a wonderful gift they are! Amen.

YOU CAN COUNT ON IT

"Do not be afraid or discouraged, for the Lord your God is with you wherever you go."

Joshua 1:9b HCSB

God has made quite a few promises to us in the Bible, and He intends to keep every single one of them.

What are some of the promises He has made to you? He will give you rest. He will provide for all your needs. He will give you strength when you feel weak. He will never leave you. Nothing can separate you from His love. And most important, He has given you eternal life through Jesus!

God's promises never fail, and they never grow old. They will always come true—you can count on it!

THOUGHT OF THE DAY

Wherever you go today, God is with you!

PRAY TODAY

Dear God, thank You for all of the promises You have made to me. Help me learn about them and always trust You. Amen.

FOLLOW THE VOICE

My sheep hear My voice, I know them, and they follow Me.

John 10:27 HCSB

Shepherds have the job of protecting, feeding, and guiding the flock of sheep that are in their care. After a while, those sheep learn to recognize the voice of their shepherd and to trust him completely. They will follow that voice wherever it goes.

The Bible tells us that Jesus is our Shepherd, and we are His sheep. Just like those other shepherds, Jesus is always protecting and caring for you. And as you get to know Jesus and learn to follow Him, you will begin to recognize His voice.

Listen closely . . . He is speaking to you!

THOUGHT OF THE DAY

The world is full of all kinds of voices—make sure you only follow your Shepherd!

PRAY TODAY

Dear God, thank You for Jesus, who is my Shepherd. Help me to always listen closely and follow where He leads me. Amen.

AN ATTITUDE OF KINDNESS

Finally, all of you should be of one mind, full of sympathy toward each other, loving one another with tender hearts and humble minds.

1 Peter 3:8 NLT

An attitude of kindness starts in your heart. Do you listen to your heart when it tells you to be kind to other people? That's always a good idea. After all, lots of people in the world aren't as fortunate as you are—and some of them are living very near you.

Ask your parents to help you find ways to do nice things for other people. And don't forget that everybody needs love, kindness, and respect. If you are always ready to share those things with others, you can make a difference wherever you go.

THOUGHT OF THE DAY

Try doing something kind for someone today. See how good it makes you feel.

PRAY TODAY

Dear God, You said that it's important to be kind. So I'll do my best to think of others and say and do things from a kind heart. Amen.

KEEP ON FORGIVING

"Rebuke your brother if he sins, and forgive him if he is sorry. Even if he wrongs you seven times a day and each time turns again and asks forgiveness, forgive him."

Luke 17:3-4 TLB

We all make mistakes, and that's why we should be quick to forgive others. But sometimes there are people in our lives who seem to need a lot of forgiveness!

Do you know someone who just keeps doing the same thing over and over, even if you've asked him or her to stop? Maybe that person has hurt your feelings or called you names, but whatever he or she has done, Jesus said we should forgive as many times as we need to.

After all, forgiveness helps you, too! So just keep on forgiving, no matter what!

THOUGHT OF THE DAY

If your feelings get hurt by a friend, don't be afraid to talk to him or her about it. That person might not realize how you feel!

PRAY TODAY

Dear God, please help me forgive as many times as I need to. Amen.

CHOOSE LIFE

I am offering you life or death, blessings or curses. Now, choose life! . . . To choose life is to love the Lord your God, obey him, and stay close to him.

Deuteronomy 30:19-20 NCV

God wants you to make good choices every day. But how can you know what choices are best?

Scripture gives us the answer: Love God, obey Him, and stay close to Him. You can do these things by talking to God often, learning what He says in the Bible, and following His teachings. As we learn more about God and do what He says, it becomes easier and easier to make the best choices. That's how we choose life every single day!

THOUGHT OF THE DAY

What are some things you have to make choices about today?

PRAY TODAY

Dear God, every day I have choices to make. Help me choose to live the way You want me to. Amen.

RESPECTFUL ACTIONS

Being respected is more important than having great riches.

Proverbs 22:1 ICB

When you treat people with respect, you show them that they are valuable. In fact, the Bible says that respect is a better gift than riches!

Being polite is an excellent way to treat others with respect. Always share, say "Please" and "Thank you," and try not to interrupt when someone is talking. If your mom or dad or a teacher asks you to do something, do it right away instead of complaining. Say a kind word to someone, or just hold the door open for the person behind you. Even the smallest respectful action can make someone's day!

THOUGHT OF THE DAY

Choose a specific way to show respect to five people today.

PRAY TODAY

Dear God, I want to be respectful. Please help me treat everyone I meet with respect. Amen.

WINNING FOR GOD

"So you want first place? Then take the last place. Be the servant of all."

Mark 9:35 MSG

The world we live in cares a lot about winning and being the very best. But the kingdom of God works a little differently.

Jesus said that if we want to be first, we have to be willing to be last and help others. If we want to really know God and follow Him, we can't always think about ourselves.

There will always be someone who needs kindness, help, or encouragement. And you can be the one to give it! You might be the very person God needs to help change someone's life. Now that's winning!

THOUGHT OF THE DAY

God always sees when you put others first—and He loves it when you do!

PRAY TODAY

Dear God, I want to be like Jesus. Help me remember that winning isn't about me—it's about serving others. Amen.

BE A HAPPY HELPER

Do everything without complaining and arguing.

Philippians 2:14 NLT

God wants us to be happy helpers. That means we should follow directions right away and without arguing.

When a parent or teacher asks you to do something, you have a choice. You can say, "Sure! I can do that!" Or you can say, "Aw, do I have to?" Which do you think would make God glad?

Following directions the first time we are asked makes everyone happier. It also shows that we are doing what God wants us to do—helping without complaining. So next time your mom or dad asks you to do something, put on a smile and be a happy helper!

THOUGHT OF THE DAY

Smile first, then respond. That's the first step to being a happy helper!

PRAY TODAY

Dear God, sometimes it's hard to follow directions. Please help me stay away from arguing so I can be happy instead. Amen!

GIVE GOD JOY

And a voice from heaven said, "You are my dearly loved Son, and you bring me great joy."

Mark 1:11 NLT

Did you know that Jesus gave God joy? As Jesus grew, He showed God's love to others. He was kind, and He obeyed God. This made God very happy.

The Bible tells us that when we trust in Jesus as our Savior, we become children of God. He loves to see all His children helping others, being kind, and learning about Him. When you do your best to be like Jesus, you will also give God joy!

THOUGHT OF THE DAY

What do you think you can do today to bring God joy?

PRAY TODAY

Dear God, please help me to be more like Jesus. I want to bring You joy too. Amen.

CHOOSE KINDNESS

Love is patient, love is kind.

1 Corinthians 13:4 HCSB

We know that kindness is always best. But if you're feeling sad or angry, you might not feel like caring for anyone else! Still, God tells us to love one another all the time. And that means acting kind even when you don't feel like it.

But here's a secret. When you do a kind act, you'll start to feel a little love! The more kind things you do, the more love you will feel. Try it out! You'll be surprised how your feelings can change when you choose kindness.

THOUGHT OF THE DAY

A kind act can be small. Who is someone you can show kindness to today?

PRAY TODAY

Dear God, help me choose kindness all the time. I want to love like You love! Amen.

WHO IS GOD?

In the same way, we can see and understand only a little about God now, as if we were peering at his reflection in a poor mirror; but someday we are going to see him in his completeness, face-to-face.

1 Corinthians 13:12 TLB

You are learning about God as you read the Bible. For instance, the Bible tells us that God loves us so much that He sent Jesus to take away our sins. And the Bible tells us that God created everything and that He can do anything!

But the Bible also says that there's a lot about God that nobody knows yet. The Bible says we'll see Him completely in heaven; but for now, we have to have faith. When you have faith, you trust that what the Bible says about God is always true, even when you don't know what He'll do next. Faith is how you grow closer to God!

THOUGHT OF THE DAY

The more you learn about God, the stronger faith you'll have. So read your Bible every day!

PRAY TODAY

Dear God, I am so grateful for what I know about You. Give me faith for what I don't understand yet. Amen.

HE LOVES YOU THAT MUCH

"For God so loved the world that he gave his only Son, so that everyone who believes in him will not perish but have eternal life."

John 3:16 NLT

Have you ever loved someone so much you were willing to do anything for him or her? God was willing to do everything for us! He held nothing back—not even His Son. That's how much God loves you!

So how big is God's love for you? It's not easy to describe or understand. But it's much bigger than anything you can imagine.

THOUGHT OF THE DAY

Can you think of three ways God shows His love for you every day?

PRAY TODAY

Dear God, I can't understand how much You love me, but I know You do. I love You, too! Amen.

SURPRISING PAYBACK

Don't repay evil for evil. Don't snap back at those who say unkind things about you. Instead, pray for God's help for them, for we are to be kind to others, and God will bless us for it.

1 Peter 3:9 TLB

When someone does something nice for you, it makes you feel good. You may want to do something nice for them, too! But what should you do when someone does or says something unkind?

God's response might surprise you. He wants you to do good to everyone, all the time! If someone says a mean thing, the best thing you can do is say something kind in return. Maybe they just need someone to show them how to be kind! It's not what everyone expects you to do. It's God's way, and God's way is always best!

THOUGHT OF THE DAY
Kindness is the best surprise of all!

PRAY TODAY
Dear God, help me surprise someone with kindness today! Amen.

QUICK TO FORGIVE

"I will forgive their sins and will no longer remember their wrongs."

Hebrews 8:12 GNT

When you say unkind words or choose not to follow the rules, it doesn't feel very good, does it? But here's some good news: You can always ask God to forgive you. And He always will!

God forgives you the moment you ask Him, and He'll fill you with His love. He will also give you courage and strength to do better the next time. His love and patience never run out. So be honest when you've made a mistake! God is always ready to forgive.

THOUGHT OF THE DAY

God forgives, no questions asked!

PRAY TODAY

Dear God, thank You that You always forgive me! When I make mistakes, help me ask for forgiveness right away. Amen.

GET IT DONE!

"All of us must quickly carry out the tasks assigned us by the one who sent me, for there is little time left before the night falls and all work comes to an end."

John 9:4 TLB

D o your parents ever ask you to pick up your toys? Do you remember to do it, or do you sometimes forget? God wants you to get your work done. He can help you with anything, even work.

We all have jobs to do, and each one is important. We should do our best to do our jobs when we are supposed to. Then you can enjoy the rest of your day and sleep peacefully at night.

THOUGHT OF THE DAY
It's so much more fun to get things done!

PRAY TODAY
Dear God, help me to do my jobs, and thank You for my fun times. Amen.

HOPE-FULL

I pray that the God who gives hope will fill you with much joy and peace while you trust in him. Then your hope will overflow by the power of the Holy Spirit.

Romans 15:13 ICB

Have you ever been so happy you can't wait to share it with someone? That's what God's hope is like! Hope comes from believing that God will always help you. Even if things don't go the way you'd like, you can have hope that God will lead you to new things He's planned just for you. That's pretty exciting! God's hope can fill you with so much joy that you'll want to share it with others. So go for it! You never know who might need to hear about God's hope.

THOUGHT OF THE DAY

When your joy overflows, share it with others!

PRAY TODAY

Dear God, I am so glad You always help me! Please show me how I can share Your hope with others. Amen.

TIME FOR GOD

Be gracious to me, Lord, for I call to You all day long.

Psalm 86:3 HCSB

Do you know that you can talk to God any time of the day or night? Some people like to pray and read their Bible in the morning. Others read Bible stories before bed. Some folks gather with friends or family to have a time called "devotions," when they read Bible verses together and talk about what they mean.

Because God is always there, you can talk, pray, or read about Him any time you want. Making time for God every day is the best way to help your faith grow and for you to become better friends with Him!

THOUGHT OF THE DAY

When do you like to spend time praying and talking with God?

PRAY TODAY

Dear God, I'm so glad I can talk to You every day. Thank You for always being there for me. Amen.

EVERYTHING YOU NEED

And my God will supply every need of yours according to his riches in glory in Christ Jesus.

Philippians 4:19 ESV

What's the difference between what you want and what you need? You might *want* a new bike, or a special toy. But what do you really *need*? You need the love of your family, food to eat, a beautiful world to enjoy, sunlight, rain, and a safe place to live. Do you know who can give you all of those things? God can! The Bible reminds us that the earth and everything in it is His! God loves you, and He takes care of everything. You don't need to worry, because God has more than enough to give you all you need.

THOUGHT OF THE DAY

Can you name some of your needs that God has already provided?

PRAY TODAY

Dear God, thank You for taking care of all my needs. I will trust You and not worry. Amen.

WHAT A BLESSING

*"But blessed are those who trust in the L*ORD *and have made the L*ORD *their hope and confidence."*

Jeremiah 17:7 NLT

Today's Bible verse says if we believe and trust in God we are blessed. But what does it mean to be blessed? Believing and trusting in God makes us feel safe and peaceful. That's being blessed. Knowing how much God loves us and sharing His love with others gives us joy. That's being blessed. Understanding that God has a wonderful plan for our life gives us peace. That's being blessed. No matter what happens around us, when we know that God is with us, we don't need to worry. We are blessed!

THOUGHT OF THE DAY

What are some ways God has blessed you?

PRAY TODAY

Dear God, thank You for always being with me, for loving me, and blessing me. Amen.

LET'S GET ALONG

Work at getting along with each other and with God.

Hebrews 12:14 MSG

Do you get along with God? If you try to follow what He says, then you probably do! Getting along with God means you spend time reading the Bible and praying, and you work hard to follow His ways.

God also wants us to get along with other people. You won't always agree with everyone, but that's OK. When you listen to others, share God's love, and help people in need, you are doing what God asks. And when you get along with others and with God, you help everyone see that God is good and loving.

THOUGHT OF THE DAY

When you get along with God, He'll help you get along with others!

PRAY TODAY

Dear God, please help me do what You want me to do. I want everyone to know how much You love us. Amen.

VISITING GOD'S HOUSE

"For where two or three are gathered together in My name, I am there among them."

Matthew 18:20 HCSB

Isn't it fun to visit a friend's house? You get to know them better and play together, too.

The Bible says that church is God's house. That makes sense! It is where you go to spend time with God and other people who are also God's children. When you go to church, you hear stories about God, sing songs about His love, and learn about the best way to live. The next time you go to church, think about all the wonderful things you can do at God's house. Then thank Him for inviting you to visit!

THOUGHT OF THE DAY

What is your favorite thing to do at church?

PRAY TODAY

Dear God, thanks for inviting me to Your house. Help me pay attention and learn everything I can about You. Amen.

CONFIDENCE FROM GOD

For the LORD will be your confidence, and will keep your foot from being caught.

Proverbs 3:26 ESV

Confidence is a big word that means "being sure you can do something." For example, once you learn how to count or spell or ride a bike, you can do those things with confidence.

But when you go to a new school, meet someone new, or try something for the first time, you might not feel very confident. That's OK, though, because the Lord says *He* will be your confidence! He is with you all the time, helping you to be brave even when you feel shy or scared. God will never let you down.

THOUGHT OF THE DAY

What is something you feel confident about? What would you like God to help you be more confident about?

PRAY TODAY

Dear God, thank You for staying close to me. Please help me trust You to give me confidence. Amen.

DO GREAT THINGS!

You are young, but do not let anyone treat you as if you were not important. Be an example to show the believers how they should live. Show them with your words, with the way you live, with your love, with your faith, and with your pure life.

1 Timothy 4:12 ICB

When we trust God, He is always with us, and we can show His love to others no matter how old we are!

God can work through you today. Is there someone you know who needs a little help? Maybe a new neighbor would like to be friends, or someone at church could use a hug. You could even ask your parents if you can give away clothes or books to kids who don't have enough. Your kind actions will show everyone that God loves us.

THOUGHT OF THE DAY

Do you have an idea that could help someone? Don't be afraid to try! Maybe your parents can help you make it happen.

PRAY TODAY

Dear God, thank You that I am important, even though I'm young. Help me do what I can to make a difference every day. Amen.

LISTEN AND ACT!

But be doers of the word and not hearers only.

James 1:22 HCSB

It's important to listen closely to the stories we hear in church. But don't stop there. The next step is to do what the Bible says!

We know from the Bible that God is happy when His people help the poor, act kindly, and tell others about His love. You can show your faith in God by doing the things He asks, and others will feel God's love through you! So the next time you hear a Bible story, try to figure out what God might be asking you to do. Then go do it!

THOUGHT OF THE DAY

Think of your favorite Bible story. What lesson can you put into action today?

PRAY TODAY

Dear God, thank You for giving me the Bible to teach me how to live. Help me be a doer of Your Word! Amen.

HAPPY THOUGHTS

Those who are pure in their thinking are happy, because they will be with God.

Matthew 5:8 NCV

Have you ever noticed that if you think about a sad story or an exciting moment, you start to feel sad or excited all over again? That's because what you think about can actually change the way you feel!

God wants us to feel joyful, so He tells us not to dwell on thoughts that make us angry or upset. Instead, think about things that come from Him, like your family, fun times with your friends, and His amazing love. That way, you will be filled with God's joy!

THOUGHT OF THE DAY

Find a happy thought for today, and hang onto it no matter what!

PRAY TODAY

Dear God, please help me think about only good things today. I want to feel Your joy! Amen.

AN ENCOURAGING WORD

So encourage each other and give each other strength.

1 Thessalonians 5:11 NCV

Sometimes the best gift you can give someone is encouragement. It's great to know our family and friends care about us, even when we're feeling down.

If your friend is feeling nervous, you could tell him all the things you like about him. If someone feels sad, you can share a funny joke or a silly story, or even just sit and listen. Don't feel like you have to solve anything. Just showing kindness and love will help someone know that you care.

THOUGHT OF THE DAY

If you notice someone feeling left out, try inviting him or her to play with you and your friends!

PRAY TODAY

Dear God, please show me how to encourage everyone around me today. Amen.

SPECIAL GIFTS

A spiritual gift is given to each of us so that we can help each other.

1 Corinthians 12:7 NLT

Everyone has a unique combination of gifts from God. Some are easy to see, like singing well or playing soccer. Others are a little harder to pick out, but they're just as important!

Do you love giving presents or teaching your friends something new? Maybe people like to talk to you when they feel sad because you're a good listener. Or maybe you enjoy telling others about God's love! Those are called "spiritual gifts." God gives you spiritual gifts so you can serve others in ways that bring joy to everyone, including yourself!

THOUGHT OF THE DAY

When you use your spiritual gifts to serve God and others, you will feel joyful!

PRAY TODAY

Dear God, please show me the gifts You've given me so I can serve You in unique and special ways! Amen.

SHINE YOUR LIGHT!

"You are like light for the whole world. A city built on top of a hill cannot be hidden."

Matthew 5:14 CEV

The Bible says that if you are a child of God, you are like a light. That means that you can help others see the right way to go just like a light can show people the way to go on a dark night.

Maybe you have a little brother or sister or a younger friend who copies what you do. It's important that you help them by being a light and showing them the right way to go. If you are kind, they will copy being kind. If you share, they will learn to share. Shine your light today!

THOUGHT OF THE DAY
What can you do to be a light for Jesus?

PRAY TODAY
Dear God, help me to be more like You so I can shine brightly. Amen.

RUMORS AND GOSSIP

Without wood, a fire will go out, and without gossip, quarreling will stop.

Proverbs 26:20 NCV

Sometimes people say unkind or untrue things about someone who isn't around. That's called gossiping, or spreading rumors. It's not nice, but you can help stop it!

Gossip can hurt people's feelings. So the next time you hear someone gossiping, try asking that person to say kind words instead. You can even go first! If you say something nice about someone, others might join in, and then gossip will give way to good friendships. And that makes God happy!

THOUGHT OF THE DAY

Make a promise to say only kind words about others. Gossip won't stand a chance!

PRAY TODAY

Dear God, thank You for warning me about gossip. Please give me kind words to say about everyone. Amen.

A STRONG VINE

"Yes, I am the Vine; you are the branches. Whoever lives in me and I in him shall produce a large crop of fruit. For apart from me you can't do a thing."

John 15:5 TLB

D o you know how grapes grow? Clusters of grapes grow on strong vines that provide everything they need. One single vine can produce lots of big, juicy grapes!

Jesus tells us that we should think of Him like a strong vine. He gives us all we need to do amazing things! We don't have to look anywhere else for love or joy or strength—Jesus has it all. So stay connected to Jesus. He'll give you an abundant life, full of His blessings!

THOUGHT OF THE DAY

You can connect to Jesus by praying, reading your Bible, and going to church!

PRAY TODAY

Dear God, thank You for being the source of everything I need. I want to stay with You forever! Amen.

GOD LOVES YOU VERY MUCH

Think how much the Father loves us. He loves us so much that he lets us be called his children, as we truly are.

1 John 3:1 CEV

God loves you unconditionally. That means that no matter what you do, God will never stop loving you. He's loved you since before you were born! He loves you when you make good choices and when you don't, and His love is the same whether you feel sad or happy or angry. God's love will never change, and you don't ever have to worry about losing it.

That kind of love can be hard to understand, but you can pray for God to reveal it to you a little more each day. It's an amazing gift!

THOUGHT OF THE DAY

God knows everything about you, and He loves you more than you know.

PRAY TODAY

Dear God, thank You for loving me no matter what! I may not understand Your love, but I trust that it never changes. Amen.

SHOW AND TELL

Here's what you do: Live well, live wisely, live humbly. It's the way you live, not the way you talk, that counts.

James 3:13 MSG

It's good to say things like "Thank you," "I'm sorry," and "I love you." But God wants us to follow those words with actions. He wants us to show *and* tell!

How can you show your love for others? Maybe you can share a favorite toy with a friend. How can you show you are thankful? What about helping your mom or dad clean up after dinner? And any time you say "I'm sorry," you can work hard to make things right. God can help you speak and act in loving ways every day!

THOUGHT OF THE DAY

Be kind in everything you say. Then be sure to act that way!

PRAY TODAY

Dear God, help me show love to everyone with both my words and my actions. Amen.

STAY IN CONTROL

Don't let your spirit rush to be angry, for anger abides in the heart of fools.

Ecclesiastes 7:9 HCSB

There is nothing wrong with feeling angry. But when we let that anger control how we act, we can make foolish choices that hurt other people.

God tells us not to get angry quickly. And He can help! When you feel yourself getting mad, stop and pray that God will help you stay in control. You can also take deep breaths or count slowly to ten. Once you've taken a little time, you'll be able to speak and act more kindly. Kind words will help the situation get better much faster than angry words!

THOUGHT OF THE DAY
Be slow to get angry and quick to be kind!

PRAY TODAY
Dear God, it's not always easy to control my angry feelings, but I know that You will help me! Amen.

LOOKING AT THE HEART

God does not see the same way people see. People look at the outside of a person, but the Lord looks at the heart.

1 Samuel 16:7 NCV

It's tempting to spend a lot of time thinking about what we look like. Sometimes it can seem like people only care about appearances. But that's not how God works! God sees who you are inside, and He loves every part of you.

Sometimes it's good to look your very best. But what you care about and how you treat people is much more important than what you look like. Don't let your out-side appearance affect how you think about yourself. Your heart is what matters to God, and He thinks you are beautiful!

THOUGHT OF THE DAY

What are some things you like about yourself?

PRAY TODAY

Dear God, thank You for looking at my heart. Help me to see others and myself like You do! Amen.

A RELUCTANT HERO

"So be strong and courageous! Do not be afraid and do not panic before them. For the Lord your God will personally go ahead of you. He will neither fail you nor abandon you."

Deuteronomy 31:6 NLT

The Bible says to be strong and brave. But it tells the story of Gideon, who didn't think he was strong and brave at all. He thought he was too small and weak to do anything for God, but God knew better. He needed Gideon to lead the army so God could save His people from an enemy. After a while, Gideon finally said yes. He trusted God and obeyed Him, and God's army won the battle.

You can trust that God knows the right plans for you, so don't be afraid. Be strong and courageous—just like Gideon!

THOUGHT OF THE DAY

God will never set you up for failure. He wants you to succeed!

PRAY TODAY

Dear God, I don't know what You have planned for me, but help me to be ready and brave when it is time. Amen.

THE GIFT OF FAITH

For by grace you have been saved through faith, and this is not your own doing; it is the gift of God.

Ephesians 2:8 NRSV

Do you know what faith is? Faith is a special kind of believing. The Bible says that faith is being sure of something that we hope for but cannot see. This means that we don't have to see something to know it is real.

What things do you believe in even though you can't see them? What about the wind? You can't see it, but you know that it is there because you can see leaves being blown about.

Faith in God is like this. Although we can't see God, we know that He is with us because we can see all that He created for us. And we can trust in God with absolute certainty.

THOUGHT OF THE DAY

God makes Himself known all around us through His creation.

PRAY TODAY

Dear God, thank You for giving me the gift of faith. Help me to see You in the world around me. Amen.

GOOD MEASURE

"Give, and you will receive. Your gift will return to you in full—pressed down, shaken together, running over, and poured into your lap. The amount you give will determine the amount you get back."

Luke 6:38 NLT

The Bible tells us that God will take care of us and that He will make sure we have everything we need. That means we shouldn't worry about the stuff we have and don't have.

Instead, God wants us to think about how we can give. For example, we can give time by helping someone, we can give kind words to someone who needs to hear them, or we can give money in an offering at church.

If you focus your attention on giving generously, God will pour out His blessings on you—more than you can possibly imagine!

THOUGHT OF THE DAY

God loves to see you giving generously to others.

PRAY TODAY

Dear God, thank You for taking care of all my needs. Help me remember to give freely and generously.
Amen.

SHARING IS BETTER

And God will generously provide all you need. Then you will always have everything you need and plenty left over to share with others.

2 Corinthians 9:8 NLT

God has promised to give you everything you need. It's a blessing to be so well taken care of.

Sometimes we forget that God is taking care of us, and we start feeling unhappy about things we don't have. We think that getting more stuff will make us happy. God wants us to trust Him and trust that He will choose to provide in just the right way. And He wants to build a generous heart in each of us so that we will want to share with others. Giving makes your heart happier!

THOUGHT OF THE DAY

Is there something you can share with someone else today?

PRAY TODAY

Dear God, thank You for taking care of me! Help me to have a generous heart. Amen.

THE LOST SHEEP

"What man among you, who has 100 sheep and loses one of them, does not leave the 99 in the open field and go after the lost one until he finds it?"

Luke 15:4 HCSB

Jesus told a story about a shepherd who had one hundred sheep. But when one wandered off, the shepherd was so worried that he could not rest. He went searching for the lost sheep, leaving the other ninety-nine sheep behind. He finally found the lost sheep, and he was so happy that he carried it all the way home.

You are just as important to Jesus as that one lost sheep was to the shepherd. Jesus told this story to show that, like a shepherd, He cares deeply about His sheep. He is our Shepherd, and we are His sheep.

THOUGHT OF THE DAY

The Lord is your Shepherd!

PRAY TODAY

Dear God, thank You for loving me so much. I love you, too. Amen.

TALKING TO GOD

I cried to him for help; I praised him with songs.

Psalm 66:17 GNT

God is always ready to hear from you. He loves for you to tell Him all about what you're feeling! And do you know that God loves to talk to you, too?

You can't hear God like you can hear another person's voice, but He's still telling you things. He might bring a new friend into your life or show you someone who needs your help. He might help you feel better when you're sad. But the best way to hear God is through the Bible. The more you learn about the Bible, the more you'll recognize God's special voice. Pretty soon, you'll hear Him everywhere!

THOUGHT OF THE DAY

Practice talking and listening to God every day. You never know what He'll say next!

PRAY TODAY

Dear God, thank You that You want to hear from me! Please help me listen for Your voice, too. Amen.

WAIT ON GOD

Wait for the LORD; be strong, and let your heart take courage; wait for the LORD!

Psalm 27:14 ESV

Over and over in the Bible, God told His people to "take courage" and wait for Him to work things out. Sometimes the heroes in the Bible had to obey God by doing really strange things like marching around Jericho seven times or fighting a battle with lamps and trumpets. But as long as they were willing to believe God, stay strong and brave, and obey Him, God always saved the day.

If you find yourself in a tough situation, be brave, and know that God will save the day for you, too!

THOUGHT OF THE DAY

God will always be faithful to you. Pray to Him, and wait and see what He will do.

PRAY TODAY

Dear God, thank You for giving me a brave heart and faith to believe You and wait on You. Amen.

ALWAYS WATCHING

"I have given you an example to follow. Do as I have done to you."

John 13:15 NLT

When other people, especially younger kids, watch what you do, what do you think they see? Do they see you being kind and patient with others, waiting your turn, and saying nice things to your friends and family?

Of course, we all make mistakes sometimes. But we have a perfect example to follow: Jesus.

You can be a good example for others to follow if you try to do what's right and treat people the way Jesus did.

THOUGHT OF THE DAY

When it's time to make a decision, ask yourself, "What would Jesus do?"

PRAY TODAY

Dear God, thank You for Jesus and for the example He set for me. Help me to be like Him. Amen.

HE HEARS YOU

"Then if my people who are called by my name will humble themselves and pray and seek my face and turn from their wicked ways, I will hear from heaven and will forgive their sins and heal their land."

2 Chronicles 7:14 NLT

God says He wants His people to be humble. That means He wants us to ask Him for help when we don't know what to do. He promises to hear us, forgive us, and help us.

Being humble also means trusting that God's ways are the best ways. He can help you through anything. Even if you have done something wrong, don't be afraid to tell God what is in your heart. He always listens, and He always loves you.

THOUGHT OF THE DAY

Take time every day to ask God what He wants you to do.

PRAY TODAY

Dear God, I know You will never leave me. Thank You for hearing my prayers and for always loving me. Amen.

ALWAYS DO WHAT'S RIGHT

So let's not allow ourselves to get fatigued doing good. At the right time we will harvest a good crop if we don't give up, or quit.

Galatians 6:9 MSG

Making right choices is always good, but sometimes it is hard to do. Maybe your friends are making a poor choice, and they want you to do the same thing. What will you do then?

It helps to remember that God loves you and is watching over you. He wants to help you do what is right, even when it's hard. Ask Him to give you courage to make good choices. He promises to surprise you with blessings when you follow Him!

THOUGHT OF THE DAY

When you need to make a choice about doing what is right, always ask God for His help.

PRAY TODAY

Dear God, I'm so glad You love me and want me to do what is right. Help me remember to call on You when I have to make hard choices. Amen.

THE POWER OF TEAMWORK

Two people are better off than one, for they can help each other succeed. If one person falls, the other can reach out and help. But someone who falls alone is in real trouble.

Ecclesiastes 4:9-10 NLT

If you have ever been on a team, you probably know how important the other members of your team are.

Can you win without the help of others? Can you throw a Frisbee to yourself? Can you defend your goal and score on your opponent at the same time? Of course not!

The Bible says that two or more can do much more together than they ever could on their own. That's why it is so important to work together with others and to be a good teammate or friend.

THOUGHT OF THE DAY

Who are your teammates and friends?

PRAY TODAY

Dear God, thank You so much for giving me good friends. Together we can do more than we ever could alone. Amen.

GOD'S STORY

I am not ashamed of the Good News, because it is the power God uses to save everyone who believes.

Romans 1:16 NCV

What are your favorite Bible stories? Maybe you love to hear about Noah's ark or David and Goliath. But guess what? The whole Bible is actually one big story about God's love for you!

The stories in the Bible show how God takes care of His people. There are also beautiful songs that praise God's powerful love, and there's lots of great advice for living the life He's planned for you. The more you read the Bible, the better you'll understand how God cares for you. You and God will become even better friends!

THOUGHT OF THE DAY

Put your Bible next to your bed so you can read something as soon as you wake up.

PRAY TODAY

Dear God, thank You for giving me Your words through the Bible. I can't wait to get to know You more! Amen.

A PURE HEART

Create in me a pure heart, God, and make my spirit right again.

Psalm 51:10 NCV

When you look at someone else what do you see? Do they have curly hair? Are they tall or short? You can only see what's on the outside, but God sees what is on the inside of each person. He sees your feelings. He knows what makes you happy or angry or afraid.

The Bible calls what is inside each person their "heart" or "spirit." When you are feeling sad or mad, your spirit doesn't feel right. The Bible says that when this happens, you can ask God to make your heart clean and your spirit right again. God cares about you, so He wants you to have a happy heart!

THOUGHT OF THE DAY

How is your heart feeling today?

PRAY TODAY

Dear God, thank You for knowing me on the inside. Please give me a pure and happy heart. Amen.

TRUE FRIENDS

A friend loves you all the time.

Proverbs 17:17 ICB

Bob and Larry have been friends for a long time! Longtime friends go through hard times, and they sometimes get annoyed, but they still stay friends. That's who God wants you to be: a true friend!

The Bible says that a true friend loves all the time. That means you keep on loving even when you're irritated or tired or when things seem really hard. True friends lift each other up in difficult times, just like God lifts you up.

So thank God for the friends in your life! And look for ways to lift them up today.

THOUGHT OF THE DAY

True friendship is a wonderful gift!

PRAY TODAY

Dear God, thank You for being the best friend of all! Help me be a true friend today and every day. Amen.

HAPPINESS AND HONESTY

Lead a quiet and peaceable life in all godliness and honesty.

1 Timothy 2:2 KJV

Have you ever said something that wasn't true? When you did, were you sorry for what you said? Probably so.

When we're dishonest, we make ourselves unhappy in surprising ways. We can feel guilty, or the truth might come out, and we end up disappointing others and God. It's not hard to see that lies always cause more problems than they solve.

But happiness and honesty go hand in hand. If you choose to be truthful, you can choose to be happy!

THOUGHT OF THE DAY

What can you do to make it easier to be truthful?

PRAY TODAY

Dear God, let me always tell the truth, even when it's hard. Amen.

NOTHING LIKE FAMILY

His unchanging plan has always been to adopt us into his own family by sending Jesus Christ to die for us. And he did this because he wanted to!

Ephesians 1:5 TLB

There is nothing like family. In fact, having loving, kind, and healthy families was always God's plan.

God knew that no family would be perfect. And that's OK. The important thing is to keep loving one another and helping one another and having one another's backs—no matter what.

What's even more exciting is that God wants all of us to be part of His own family, and that's why He sent Jesus. There's nothing better than that!

THOUGHT OF THE DAY

The Bible says God has adopted you into His family. Ask your parents about adoption and what it means.

PRAY TODAY

Dear God, I am so glad to be part of Your family. You are my Heavenly Father, and I love You. Amen.

ANYTHING IS POSSIBLE

Jesus replied, "Why do you say 'if you can'? Anything is possible for someone who has faith!"

Mark 9:23 CEV

Whatever your dream may be—for now or in the future—anything is possible!

What others say about you, or even what you think about yourself, is not what you should count on. Instead, believe what God says about you! And God says in the Bible that anything is possible with Him. He's got great plans for you! And God never quits or gives up on you.

Put your faith in God, and believe that He wants what's best for you!

THOUGHT OF THE DAY

What's your dream? Do you talk to God about it?

PRAY TODAY

Dear God, You said anything is possible with faith. So I am going to keep my faith in You. Amen.

STICK TOGETHER

How good and how pleasant it is when God's people live together in unity!

Psalm 133:1 NIV

The Bible tells us it is important to live in unity with others. Living in unity means that we work together as a team, and each person contributes in his or her own way. When we do this, we are better able to handle challenges when they happen.

Your family succeeds when you work as a team. No basketball or football team will do well if all the players do their own thing! The same is true for you and your family—whether in good times or in bad, if you stick together, the results will be amazing!

THOUGHT OF THE DAY
How can you help someone in your family today?

PRAY TODAY
Dear God, please help me remember to be kind to my family and do my part so we can help one another. Amen.

A HAPPY SMILE

A glad heart makes a cheerful face.

Proverbs 15:13 ESV

Has someone's smile or laugh ever made you smile or laugh too? Your smile can do the same for other people. Sometimes a smile can help someone who is feeling unhappy to feel better.

God made you to be happy and smile every day. Start by asking God to help you remember all of the great things He has done and all that you have to be thankful for. Then, once your heart is happy, your face can't help but be happy too! Your happiness will be contagious!

THOUGHT OF THE DAY

Nothing says "God loves you!" quite like a happy smile!

PRAY TODAY

Dear God, thank You for giving me a glad and cheerful heart. Help me to always remember Your goodness to me. Amen.

RUN TO FINISH WELL

Let us run the race that is before us and never give up.

Hebrews 12:1 NCV

Have you ever run in a race? Some races are short and other races are long, but every race has a finish line. In order to finish well, you need to keep running. If you quit, you won't get there!

The Bible says that life is a lot like a race. Some things take a short time—like helping at home or finishing homework. Other things take a long time—like learning to read or playing a sport. Just like in a race, you need to keep going in order to finish well!

THOUGHT OF THE DAY

What is something you'd like to get better at doing?

PRAY TODAY

Dear God, thank You for always being with me and helping me to finish well. Amen.

TURN YOUR FROWN UPSIDE DOWN!

A cheerful look brings joy to the heart; good news makes for good health.

Proverbs 15:30 NLT

Have you ever noticed how being around a frowning person can make you feel sad too? But what happens when you are around a smiling person?

The Bible reminds us that we can share our happiness with others. And when we belong to Jesus, we have lots to smile about! We know that He loves us and will never leave us. We know that He hears our prayers. We know that every good thing we have comes from Him. When you think of all your blessings, it's easy to turn a frown upside down into a smile. Try it! You'll feel better, and so will everyone around you!

THOUGHT OF THE DAY

Think about a time when someone's smile made you feel better.

PRAY TODAY

Dear God, when I'm feeling sad, please help me remember all the ways You show me You love me. Amen.

SAYING THANKS

Praise the Lord. Give thanks to the Lord, for he is good; his love endures forever.

Psalm 106:1 NIV

When your mom or dad does something nice for you, you probably say thanks! When a friend shares a toy or gives you a gift, you say thanks, too. But have you ever thought about saying thanks to God?

He is always good, He loves you, and He gives you wonderful things every day! God gives you family and friends, good food to eat, and a beautiful world where you can run and play. It makes God happy when His children take the time to say thanks for all He does. Will you do that today?

THOUGHT OF THE DAY
Think of three things you can thank God for right now!

PRAY TODAY
Dear God, thank You for loving me and for helping me every day. Amen.

GROWING FAITH

So faith comes from hearing, that is, hearing the Good News about Christ.

Romans 10:17 NLT

The Scripture verse above says that faith, or believing, comes from hearing the Good News about Jesus. There are lots of ways to do that!

Maybe you go to Sunday school or church, where you listen to Bible stories and learn songs that tell you about God's love. When you read a devotional book like this one, you are also hearing the Good News. Reading the Bible and saying prayers before you eat or at bedtime help grow your faith too! Every day, try finding a few ways to help your faith get stronger and stronger.

THOUGHT OF THE DAY

What is your favorite way to learn about Jesus?

PRAY TODAY

Dear God, thank You for giving me so many ways to hear about Jesus and Your love for me! Please help my faith grow. Amen.

SHARE WHAT YOU HAVE

Do not neglect to do good and to share what you have, for such sacrifices are pleasing to God.

Hebrews 13:16 ESV

Nobody has everything. But everybody has something! And when we share the things we have, everyone can enjoy a little more.

God asks us to share the things we have. Think about all the things you can share with others! When you play with a friend, you can share your toys so you'll both have more fun. If someone at school doesn't have a snack, you can ask if they want to share yours. Sharing makes people feel loved and cared for. And that makes God happy, too!

THOUGHT OF THE DAY

Think of a time someone shared something with you. How did that make you feel?

PRAY TODAY

Dear God, please show me the things I can share with others. Then help me share them joyfully! Amen.

SING TO THE LORD!

Shout with joy to the LORD, all the earth! Worship the LORD with gladness. Come before him, singing with joy.

Psalm 100:1-2 NLT

D o you like to sing? Have you ever felt so happy that you just had to sing a song? Singing, playing musical instruments, clapping your hands, and dancing are all wonderful ways to show your joy!

When we see the beautiful world God has created and all the ways God has blessed us with family and friends, sometimes our joy just bubbles out! So when you're happy and you know it, shout for joy! God loves to hear how glad you are to be His child.

THOUGHT OF THE DAY

What is your favorite song about Jesus?

PRAY TODAY

Dear God, thank You for making me Your child and giving me so many good things. Help me celebrate You today! Amen.

THINKING LIKE JESUS

Make your own attitude that of Christ Jesus.

Philippians 2:5 HCSB

The way you think is called your "attitude." The Bible says we should try to have the same attitude as Jesus. We can know how Jesus thought by listening to stories about Him and reading what He said in the Bible. Jesus loved others and said they were important. Jesus didn't worry about things because He trusted God to give Him all He needed. Jesus looked for what was good, even when things didn't go the way He wanted. And guess what? You can choose to think the same way Jesus did!

THOUGHT OF THE DAY

Things look brighter every day when you think the "Jesus way"!

PRAY TODAY

Dear God, please help me have a Jesus attitude. I want to learn to think more like Him. Amen.

GIFTS FROM GOD

God has given each of you a gift from his great variety of spiritual gifts. Use them well to serve one another.

1 Peter 4:10 NLT

What do you love to do? Do you enjoy telling stories or playing sports or playing music? Or maybe you can't wait to play with animals or learn about science!

No matter what you do, give thanks to God. God gives each of us special gifts and abilities, which are sometimes called "talents." Think about what your talents might be and then work hard to get better at them! When you do, God can use you in amazing ways to serve others and share His love. And that's the greatest gift of all!

THOUGHT OF THE DAY

How can you use your talents to serve others?

PRAY TODAY

Dear God, thank You for the talents You've given me. Help me work hard so You can do great things through me! Amen.

KNOW IT BY HEART

Mom or Dad, help your son memorize this verse
and talk to him about what it means.

*Rejoice always, pray continually,
give thanks in all circumstances;
for this is God's will for you
in Christ Jesus.*

—

1 Thessalonians 5:16-18 NIV

Mom or Dad, help your son memorize this verse
and talk to him about what it means.

*Listen to what is wise
and try to understand it.*

—

Proverbs 2:2 GNT

KNOW IT BY HEART

Mom or Dad, help your son memorize this verse
and talk to him about what it means.

*With God's power working in us,
God can do much, much more than
anything we can ask or think of.*

—

Ephesians 3:20 ICB

KNOW IT BY HEART

Mom or Dad, help your son memorize this verse
and talk to him about what it means.

*Love is patient and kind.
Love is not jealous, it does not brag,
and it is not proud.*

—

1 Corinthians 13:4 ICB

KNOW IT BY HEART

Mom or Dad, help your son memorize this verse
and talk to him about what it means.

*"Sovereign LORD, you made the earth and
the sky by your great power and might;
nothing is too difficult for you."*

—

Jeremiah 32:17 GNT

Mom or Dad, help your son memorize this verse
and talk to him about what it means.

The LORD's love never ends.
His mercies never stop.
They are new every morning.
LORD, your loyalty is great.

—

Lamentations 3:22-23 ICB

KNOW IT BY HEART

Mom or Dad, help your son memorize this verse
and talk to him about what it means.

*I will be glad and rejoice in you;
I will sing the praises
of your name, O Most High.*

—

Psalm 9:2 NIV

Mom or Dad, help your son memorize this verse
and talk to him about what it means.

*Don't worry about anything,
but in all your prayers ask God
for what you need, always asking him
with a thankful heart.*

—

Philippians 4:6 GNT

Mom or Dad, help your son memorize this verse
and talk to him about what it means.

*See how very much our Father loves us,
for he calls us his children,
and that is what we are!*

—

1 John 3:1-3 NLT

KNOW IT BY HEART

Mom or Dad, help your son memorize this verse
and talk to him about what it means.

The Lord your God
wins victory after victory
and is always with you.
He celebrates and sings because of you,
and he will refresh your life with his love.

—

Zephaniah 3:17 CEV

KNOW IT BY HEART

Mom or Dad, help your son memorize this verse
and talk to him about what it means.

*Be kind to each other, tenderhearted,
forgiving one another,
just as God through Christ
has forgiven you.*

—

Ephesians 4:32 NLT